Opening To Your Intuition
and Psychic Sensitivity
Developing Your Sixth Sense

BOOK THREE

By Elizabeth Joyce

Opening to Your Intuition and Psychic Sensitivity

Developing Your Sixth Sense

BOOK THREE

Opening to Your Intuition and Psychic Sensitivity
Developing Your Sixth Sense
BOOK THREE

ISBN-10:— 0615928218
ISBN-13:— 978-0-6159282-1-0

Cover Artist: Jim Warren
Cover Art Copyright by Jim Warren.
www.jimwarren.com/site/
Email:jim@jimwarren.com

Publishing, Editing, and Page Layout by
Visions of Reality
Chalfont, PA 18914

Visions of Reality books may be ordered through Amazon.com, Ingram, booksellers, or by contacting:

Visions of Reality
PO Box 128
Chalfont, PA 18914
www.new-visions.com
215-996-0646

Printed in the United States of America

ALSO BY ELIZABETH JOYCE

Books
Psychic Attack, Are You A Victim?

Ascension—Accessing The Fifth Dimension

*Ascension—Accessing The Fifth Dimension
Workbook*

*Opening To Your Intuition and Psychic Sensitivity
Developing Your Sixth Sense
BOOK ONE
And
BOOK TWO*

CD Programs
*Spiritual Healing and Meditation
Healing Depression the Natural Way
The Chakras and Your Body
Opening The Spiritual Chakras
Inserting the Divine Seals
Distant Healing with the Divine Seals*

All of the above items are available from
Amazon.com, Ingram, Book Stores,
BBSRadio.com/letsfindout, and
Visions of Reality
at
www.new-visions.com

This work is dedicated to
the energetic and natural healing centers
around the world as well as all
Teachers of Light.

Allow the various chapters to help you open
your heart, tune in, and learn the ways
of the other realms, dimensions, and worlds.

It doesn't always work. But when it does,
and it usually does,
It is more powerful than parts
From which it is made.

This knowledge is now being passed
along to you.

TABLE OF CONTENTS

ACKNOWLEDGEMENTS

First, my thanks goes to Margaret Stettner, Indira Ivey, William Vitalis, Dr. Frank Alper, Louise Hay, and Dr. Deepak Chopra, who gave me the thoughts for these classes and the courage to begin the teaching.

Next, I thank every student who took these classes over the years. May the lessons remain with you and help you guide your life in harmony with the Divine.

I thank Evelyn Hart for her complete dedication to each and every original graphic in this book. She has a sense of knowing exactly what I am picturing, and getting it down on paper. Thanks again, ever so much, Evelyn.

Most important, to *the Invisible Teachers* and the higher energies, I bow in reverence, gratitude, and surrender.

Opening To Your Intuition and Psychic Sensitivity

Developing Your Sixth Sense

BOOK THREE

INTRODUCTION

Over the past thirty years or so I have been blessed to open up to my *Inner Self* of intuition and inner guidance, which has been an invaluable and priceless gift. There have been many earthly teachers guiding me along the way, beginning with Grammie Hemphill, Meg Stettner, Indira Ivie, William Vitalis, Louise Hay, Dr. Frank Alper, Dr. Deepak Chopra, Mark Tremblay, Dr. Joseph Schor, and many others. However, my inner angels and guides have been a lively and actively sharing part of this incarnation as well.

The lessons have been many and the rewards greater one can put into words. It was Meg who asked me to begin to teach this work to others. Meg knew the importance and truth that came from so many people with similar experiences. I have continually been fascinated by those who told their truth and stated that their lives were transformed through the catalyst of blending with intelligence beyond this planet Earth.

Mankind has always believed in unseen intelligence inhabiting an invisible world, of lives and existences within the other realms. The Holy Books of many religious beliefs support these ideas and inform their followers that such a Spiritual existence vibrates in close proximity to our own world. According to Biblical tradition, Angels stand by, ready to guide, support, and defend mankind against dangers of life on the earth plane. In addition, Angels have charge of the dead.

We are on the threshold of a new time, a new era of enlightenment, peace and calm. Today the Spiritual matrix surrounding our planet Earth holds a much stronger energetic vibration, which brings a broader vision. *As complete envelopment into the Fifth Dimension arrived and this new, powerful Spiritual energy must integrate with the physical body if we are to survive.*

What occurred on December 21, 2012, brought in the new vibration, emanating from the Double Helix in the center of our galaxy. This vibrational force entered and began to raise the consciousness of life on this planet and entire Solar System. The energetic vibration lasted for seventy-two hours.

It is known as creating the zero point. The physical body and mind merged with the invisible realms of the eternal, while at the same time maintaining an *unalterable course* toward Spiritual enlightenment.

On December 21, 2012, a rare celestial alignment culminated, aligning the galactic center with our Solar System. At this point, the Winter Solstice Sun aligned with the center of the Milky Way Galaxy, the home of our Solar System, together with at least 200 billion other stars, creating a "sky portal" in the "dark rift" of the Milky Way.

The morphogenetic quality began on December 23rd, at the end of the 72 hours of vibrational force. This era will be known as *"Galactic Synchronization."* A new galactic cycle began in 1999, and we will continue to see accelerated changes in predictable directions until 2031, when another new galactic cycle will begin on January 23, 2031, leading to Universal consciousness and the end of linear history. (Chinese New Year of the Pig)

We have a lot of inner work to do before this predestined date ascends upon us. Man is indeed the creator of his own reality, but not as a separate force. There is too much he cannot discover or begin to understand until he flows with the Universal energy of the Divine. He must dispel his own illusion of sole importance in the Universe and accept the reality of a valid and essential attachment to all life through accessing the complete Spiritual matrix of the Universe.

Man is not, and has never been, except by his own choice, rooted to a simple completion of a preordained growth cycle. Instead, he is free to creatively blend the physical and the Spiritual matrices, allowing the body and mind freedom to fulfill their life patterns. This is what defines free will. This is the search for the question we always ask, *"Who am I?"*

The new science, Quantum Physics, is bringing man back to using the intuitive, back to an inter-galactic reality. For with every mystery that is explainable there are five that are not. Individuals now feel closer to the vastness, the great majesty of the unexplainable. They are less threatened by the possibility of an emptiness or obliqueness after death. The awesomeness of this unsolved puzzle...*do we have life after death?* is helping the human race suspend the illusion of sole importance in order to recognize the need of joining all the life forces.

We are returning to Atlantean energies, its buried Spiritual matrix, and perhaps beyond that. Much of the old heirarchy ways will become unearthed and put back into practice. Along with our invisible guides and angels, the new Fifth Dimension energies, and the connection to all things (Oneness) we will walk the path of harmony and peace. This is the only true way the individual and collective consciousness has of becoming healed and whole.

Your cells not only have a biomechanical structure, which creates your physical body; they also energetically control and link your emotional reactions to events that continually occur in your life.

The intensity of one's thoughts and actions can write an energetic blueprint, *Akashic Record*, similar to a computer program, which magnetically attracts people, events, situations, and experiences to you. *Opening to Your Intuition—Book Three* brings you exercises, new thoughts, and precise explanations of how to attract, proceed and enter into the new energies with balance.

How this is Affecting Your Life Right Now

You are your own creator. If you find that areas of your life are unbalanced, dysfunctional or out of control and you've tried numerous self help methods in the past, but have failed to break out of destructive patterns, and you wonder why the same type of issues repeat themselves time and time again, then your *Cellular Memory Structure* could be the reason.

Your cells are your *genetic family tree*. Past generations of family members have left their own imprint in your cellular memory. Some of the responses, characteristics or actions you have in life have evolved through the genetic-key make up originating from the beginning of your family time-line. This is what Spirit says we call 'original sin'.

Some organ transplant recipients have been reported to show characteristics of the person who donated the organ. This further identifies that there is a direct relationship between one cellular memory family and another. The scientific community is yet to discover the full implications of the cells' abilities. However, from a Spiritual perspective, it was predicted that there would be a scientific break-through that would throw light onto the relevance of the cells and that ground-breaking technologies would evolve from this knowledge. (Read the *Ascension—Accessing The Fifth Dimension WORKBOOK* for detailed information.)

In these pages we will look at the higher energies. *Book One* introduced us to *Metaphysics*, the invisible energies and their initial use. *Book Two* brings in the ways to work with and strengthen these energies. *Book Three* teaches you, once you have built up your body and Spiritual strength, how to work with these forces safely.

You will work with the new Frequencies, past, present, and future lives, your personal Guides and Angels, the new Spiritual Chakras and Divine Seals, your Akashic Records, the powerful Circe of Light, learn how to manifest, and about your Soulmate.

The writing of this book is motivated by many people who have asked me how to build up and strengthen their intuition and live a peaceful existence, free from fear. Each chapter has a description and checklist of how best to access the energies described within. What strategies, meditations, prayers, and exercises one can use to tap into the higher realms, receive news from their departed loved ones, or to understand their emotional pain and experiences on this planet, is explained. We can always bring love to any situation and work from a love based center instead of worries, doom, gloom, the ego, or fear.

It is suggested that you include all three books in your library. Together they bring you the completion of a process. You will gain the knowledge and awareness of how the cycle of life works, and be able to continue on your personal path, while maintaining good physical, mental-emotional, and Spiritual health.

May these pages enlighten you, open up your higher knowledge, and guide you to walk the path of *Love, Peace, and Harmony*.

—Elizabeth Joyce
November 22, 2013
Chalfont, PA

Opening to Your Intuition—Book Three

CHAPTER ONE

Review — White Light and The Chakras

First let's take a look at the Seven Physical Chakras – then we can learn how to use them, help them clear and spin in balance, to keep us healthy while aligning us with the energy of the Divine.

1. The ROOT Chakra – located at the base of the Spine

COLOR – RED
Rules the Kidneys and the Spinal Column –

Sutras: Foundation, Security, Strength

Holds the Kundalini energy for meditation. Vitalizes the Kidneys and feeds the life giving system – the will to live – and the fundamental instincts for survival. Stores our Chi energy.

Crystal: Jasper, Clear Quartz

For grounding: Kundalini energy is stored here, transformation can occur when these energies are aroused and allowed to rise up within you and penetrate each Chakra above. The energy joins the Shakti energy at the Heart Center, continues on and leaves the body through the top of the head – or Crown Chakra. As this happens, Spiritual growth and awareness of other levels of energy and perceptions occur.

2. The SPLEEN Chakra – Located at the Spleen between the hipbones.

COLOR – ORANGE
Rules Gonads, Sexual Organs, Sacral – Lower back – **Sutras:** Purification, Receiving, Creativity

Located between the Asis bones of the hips. Vitalizes the sexual life organs of reproduction and processes prana (or oxygen) from the atmosphere, which then vitalizes the entire system of major and minor Chakras.

Crystal: Topaz, Carnelian

For health, sexual energies, digestion, and purification. This energy can be used for creativity, Spiritual awareness and integration. It also influences our self-esteem.

3.   The SOLAR PLEXUS Chakra – The largest Chakra on the body – Located at the navel

COLOR – GREEN
Rules the Pancreas – Adrenals – Stomach – Gall Bladder – Nervous System – **The Sutras:** Will, Integrity, Desire, Intention

Vitalizes the sympathetic nervous system, which activates our involuntary muscles and gets the body ready for activity. (Adrenaline) This Chakra can bring to us joy, sadness, gut feeling reactions and heightens emotion.

Crystal: Emerald, Black Obsidian

This is the male creative force or YANG energy in the body. It brings to us our desires, other people, and controls our emotions and physical power. The Solar Plexus energy helps to create our future and causes us to have our gut feeling reactions; or; psychic impressions;. When out of balance or holding negative energy, it can cause us to think and act in unhealthy ways.

Creates the possibilities of choices. What are the consequences of my actions and how will they be affected? Take a different choice than your conditioned response by following your intuition and integrity. Witness your body's energies – do you feel comfortable or uncomfortable? When we choose actions that bring happiness to others the energy that returns to us is happiness and success. This is a very important Chakra and houses our will, intention and integrity, as well as our "gut feeling reactions."

4.   THE HEART CENTER – Located at the Heart

COLOR – YELLOW

Rules the Thymus – Circulatory System – Blood – **Sutras:** Love, Peace, Harmony, Laughter

Vitalizes the life stream through the pumping of the heart center, and controls the circulation of the blood. The heart feeds all cells within the body structure. Vitalizes the veges nerve, the largest nerve in the parasympathetic nervous system. When open it helps us remove fear blocks, and brings compassion in the form of Spiritual love. Through our Heart Chakra we can feel a connection and sense of oneness with others.

Crystal: Rose Quartz, Amber
Unconditional Love, self-acceptance, and the place where Spirit can guide us to higher levels of being and loving. The heart is the Mother in all of us. Kindness, Forgiveness, Love, Peace and Harmony.

5.   THE THROAT CHAKRA – Located at the Throat Center

COLOR – BLUE

Rules the Thyroid, parathyroid – Alimentary Canal – Lungs – **Sutras:** discernment, affluence, acceptance.

Located at the base of the Throat, between the shoulder blades. Vitalizes the lungs and voice. Communicates the concrete thoughts received from the Solar Plexus.

Crystal: Sapphire, Turquoise

Self-expression, communication, affluence, discernment.

This is the Mother Chakra and begins the three YIN or female energy chakras of the body. You can inflict pain or kindness with the voice. What is more important to know is the voice represents our intention. We will decree a thing and it will be so. Therein lies the mystery of manifestation. As Louise Hay states in the book *You Can Heal Your Life*, where thoughts go, energy flows; Our life experiences comes directly from our thoughts, then speaking it, then our actions. Inherent within every intention and desire is the mechanics for its fulfillment. The voice had great organizing.

6.   THE THIRD EYE CHAKRA –
Located at the center of the Brow Ridge

COLOR-INDIGO
Rules the Pituitary – Left Eye – Nose – **Sutras:** Knowledge, Wisdom, Freedom

Vitalizes the cerebellum (or lower brain) and central nervous system, which consist of the brain fibers connected at the base of the brain and top of the spinal cord—or 9th Chakra, and anchors the conscious stream from the etheric body.

Crystal: Ruby, Lapis
Knowledge, truth, freedom of the etheric double, intuition.

The Third Eye helps you to see all circumstances around you, and is the key to wisdom and controlling/directing the Life Force energies. While meditating and working the chakra energies, colors, pictures, feelings and an inner knowing will come to you through the Third Eye. This is the ultimate power center for healing others, and allows you to Astral Project or work with your etheric body (your double) at will.

7.   THE CROWN CENTER CHAKRA – Located at the top center of the Head

COLOR – VIOLET-WHITE-SILVER
Rules the Pineal – Connects to 8th Chakra – 6 inches above the head – Right Eye – **Sutras:** Bliss, Infinity, Immortality

Vitalizes the cerebrum (or upper brain) and anchors the etheric stream into the physical body. It is the direct connection to our Higher Self and brings reverence, knowledge of Infinity, insights from the Spiritual Self – or Etheric Double and brings dedication to God from the Spiritual Will.

Crystal: Diamond

Immortality, Angels, Grace, Communing with the Divine Forces, Self-Realization.

Through the Crown Chakra you can literally reach the heavens or other energy realms. You can rise through the center of your head and astral travel with your Guides. You can project healing, and pure, unconditional love energies anywhere in the Universe. This is where the power of prayer becomes reinforced. This is the center where you bring in the Spiritual Forces through Shakti Energy to purify the body and join the kundalini energies in order to reach a nirvana or total purification and recalibration of the cellular structure and DNA system of the body. You can erase karma through

Divine Grace brought through the Crown Chakra into the Heart Center.

THE CHAKRA SYSTEM

In viewing the Seven Chakra system, the colors appear from the first Chakra (Root) to the seventh Chakra (Crown), in a specific order. This should be very familiar to you as they are identical to the colors of the rainbow, except that the green and yellow vibrations are switched. Each color expresses a range of frequencies that fall within specific wavelengths of radiant information. The colors of the visible light system are just above Infrared and below Ultraviolet.

The Chakras are specifically designed to act as one level of a tuning antenna, aligned with a note on the scale of seven. They intercept specific wavelengths of energy containing radiant information and bring that information down into the density of the body structure to utilize. Additionally, more refined tuning occurs at the molecular level, as genetic receptors receive information at an even greater level of vibration frequency.

The spin rate of the Chakras is a part of the fine-tuning of this system. The higher chakras spin faster than the lower ones. There is a direct relationship between each individual chakra center and the specific ranges of energy within the human/creation Matrix. The chakra is the interface point, the energetic organ linking various aspects of the physical body to its non-physical counterparts...i.e. the Matrix Grid.

Through this resonate relationship you have access to the entire range of creation, an Infinite Grid, of information can be accessed through the body/chakra system. Using the interface points of the Chakras, you become a living, vibrating part of all that you see!

Opening to the Eighth Chakra
with the Divine Seals

Sagittarius

Taurus

Crown
Center

8th

Aquarius

Third
Eye

7th

8-1/2th

6th

Pisces

Throat
Chakra

9th

Leo

E=MC(2)

5th

Heart
Center

4th

Capricorn

Solar
Plexis

Scorpio

3rd

Cancer

Spleen
Chakra

2nd

1st

0
Beyond

0

Root
Chakra

Foot
Chakra

Aries

Virgo

(EH)

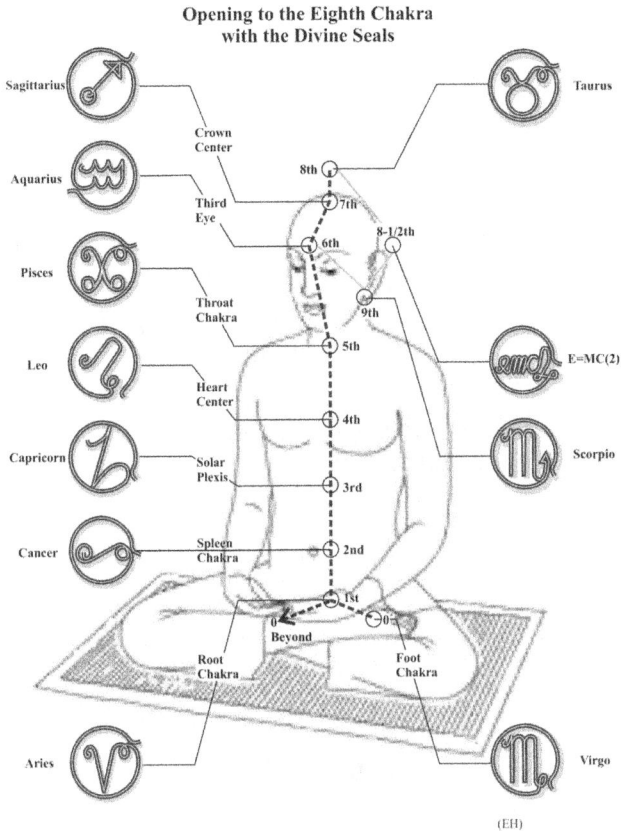

THE CHAKRAS AND DIVINE SEALS

TO THE 8th CHAKRA

Which is eight feet above your
Crown Center

The new Spiritual Chakras are described
in Chapter VI

For Example

The seventh chakra, associated with the pineal gland, interfaces with an Infinite Grid of radiant energy – information – light frequency – as well as a higher HOLOGRAPHIC expression of itself as a pineal gland. It is through this interface that the reality of the human experience becomes apparent. The human being is not the individual and independent being, as we perceive. Rather, it is a continuation of energy seeking expression through multiple energy vortexes of expression. The body is connected to one level of an interlocking series of grids, connected to the Hierarchy, with each system sustaining its own range of energy information. These grids, having seven sections or sets of vibrations, with seven levels of knowledge in each section, are ranges of experience referred to as Dimensions.

In aging or illness, the Chakras begin to collapse into the body and slow their rate of spinning. The ancients knew of this and designed rites or rituals of mantras and meditation techniques to maintain the vitality and spin-rate of the chakras. Recommended as a daily meditation practice, these movements are not aerobic in nature; through they may be performed quickly and are used in Tibetan Monasteries as a mode of prayer, meditation and physical maintenance.

The radiant energy of creation penetrates to you and within you on a daily basis, incessantly. Wave packets of information, coded as geometric patterns of subtle energy carried upon waves of a broad spectrum of light contain knowledge and insight along with ideas and creativity – through Light! Every second of every day you are asked to process this information, determine what is useful to you and what is not, and store what is useful in a portion of your mind, body, spirit complex where the pattern of the memory will reside. Much passes by you, and much is absorbed as you grow along your personal time line and open up to the Matrix Grid. Any and all knowledge is accessible to you, instantaneously.

The key here is to remember that the body may not use all wavelengths of energetic information; each chakra, through its individual spin rate, is in tune to vibrate within a specific range of frequency. These frequencies determine which portions of Light are meaningful to your vibration rate and growth. The chakras, and the associated grids, respond only to the information to which they are tuned, allowing all remaining information to pass. It is through the resonant receptors of the genetic code that the body, individually and as a species, is able to tune into the chakras, and access the living information of Light as it passes through the body All information of creation is available to you. The information may not be meaningful, however, until we are able to bring it in to the body through the re-tuning of the Chakras on a regular basis.

Individuals learn to assimilate information, unconsciously and the information is received through the Hierarchy of the subtle bodies.

The system, overwhelmed by the sheer volume of the information, begins to temporarily store data within the buffer zone for the body to access and use at a later time.

The buffer zones will continue to store the information until they reach saturation and can hold no more. At this point, the buffer zones are vibrating as a specific tone that moves into resonance with the sleep centers of the brain, releasing serotonin and inducing a need to sleep within the body.

The sleeping process allows the body to process and empty the information accumulated within the buffer zone, and assimilates the energy into the Matrix Grid of the body. To the places where the life experience dictates that the information should fit. The fittings will change throughout the lifetime, as new experiences will allow for re-evaluation of previous experiences and a re-organization as to how they should fit into the system and life patterns.

As the body learns to vibrate differently, resonating into the higher Matrix Grids of information, the body will require less sleep. You may be experiencing this in your life at the present time. Collectively and individually, you have already learned to vibrate much more rapidly than you did even last year. Initially, as you learn the chakra system and begin to work with the meditations, the sudden increase in cellular vibration may be accompanied by a perceived need for more sleep, especially if deep seeded emotions have been awakened. It is always best to allow for the extra need for sleep as it occurs. This need for extra sleep will dissipate as the body settles into the new patterns of vibration and assimilation of information.

This process of opening your Chakras may be seen as a double-edged sword. As the emotions become dislodged, forgotten and sometimes painful memories begin to surface. The higher vibration of experience will allow for them to be resolved quickly, and this resolution restores balance, or healing. The increase in vibration allows chakras to rotate at a faster rate and process the information in instant time as they are occurring. The net effect of this, living in the moment, is that the body will be asked to store less and demand less sleep time to process your daily events.

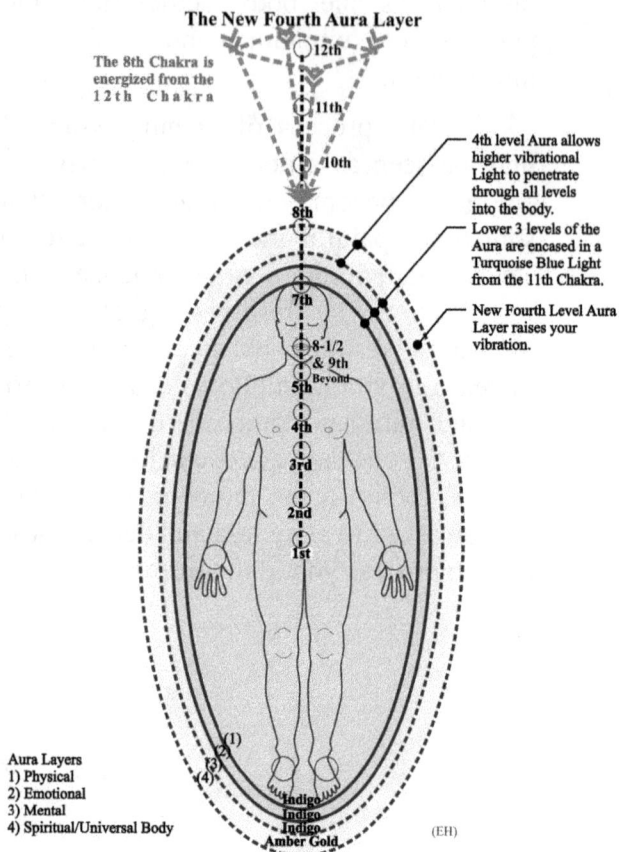

The New Fourth Aura Layer

The 8th Chakra is energized from the 12th Chakra

12th

11th

10th

8th

4th level Aura allows higher vibrational Light to penetrate through all levels into the body.

Lower 3 levels of the Aura are encased in a Turquoise Blue Light from the 11th Chakra.

New Fourth Level Aura Layer raises your vibration.

7th

8-1/2 & 9th Beyond

5th

4th

3rd

2nd

1st

Aura Layers
1) Physical
2) Emotional
3) Mental
4) Spiritual/Universal Body

(1)
(3)
(4)

Indigo
Indigo
Indigo
Amber Gold

(EH)

THE AURA SHIELD

As discussed in *Book One*, the AURA Shield is what protects you from the forces, both seen and unseen. A miraculous Spiritual force operates within us, around us, and beyond us. Although invisible to the individual eye, it is energetic, vividly alive and full of color. This field is a part of us and we are a part of it –

commonly known as *the human energy field or aura*. The Aura is defined as *"a subtle, invisible essence or fluid said to emanate from human and animal bodies, and even from inanimate objects; a psychic electro-mental effervescence surrounding a person; character, personality."*

It is well established that all activity of our human body is associated with electric currents, which circulate through the organs, and actually form a definite *electrical field* around us. Scientists have perfected apparatus that can detect this very field of force, which exists around every living thing. The presence of this field can extend more than twenty-five miles from the body in some instances. This is not the same as static electricity that can be felt when we put on nylon gloves or something similar, as a mild electrical shock. This is quite different. We have a biological electrical force field that may be considered and the first and densest of several layers of force fields which make up the composite emanation, which we call the *aura*.

The two aspects of consciousness, emotions and the mind, are closely linked together, and the energies of the inner worlds stream through the bodies, which is our means of contact with the other, outer words. This is what happens when we meditate and receive telepathy and guidance from our Blessed Higher Self. These energies also radiate out and around the physical body, but extend over a larger area than the vital energy of our etheric double. This energy field has been labeled as your *charisma*. Whereas the extent of this vital radiation can usually be stated in inches, the combined emotional-mental radiation extends for several feet in the average person, and in more highly developed people it will exceed this.

The Spiritual aura extends beyond the body and varies from a few feet, in the case of un-evolved people, to yards or even miles in the case of highly developed people. It is taught that the Spiritual aura of Lord Buddha extended for two hundred miles, and Buddha taught us that this entire planet, as well as the solar system is held in the aura of a very great being. This is also a Christian teaching: St. Paul said, *"In Him we live and move and have our being."*

There is a part of the aura, the first quarter-inch to half-inch that is called *the mysterious dark space*. This area has electrical forces flowing through it, and is believed to be where the body repels or rejects energy. However, not much had been discovered about this space.

It is important to realize that the aura is at all times registering the general emotional and mental quality of one's consciousness. This quality is something that is relatively stable and is based on a long-term and continuing series of emotional and mental habits of the conscious mind. So, like attracts like, we are what we think and we become what we eat. The result of this activity gives the aura a general coloring which changes, although somewhat slowly. This coloring gives the psychic a clear indication of the physical, mental and emotional character of the client. A good psychic reader of auras can determine, from the various appearances of the aura, the actions, thoughts, and emotions of the client.

The aura has two definite aspects. There is the form and shape of the aura, as well as the colorful emanations that surround the physical body. The colorful currents are considered a magnetic force field through which the finer substances of the inner levels of manifestation are continually flowing.

After December 21, 2012, a new layer to our aura developed. This is called the fourth level to the aura and its color is Amber. It is thought that this layer holds the powerful higher Fifth Dimension energies and is used to raise our consciousness as well as to strengthen and protect us.

As you work through the lessons within this book, Level Three of *Opening Your Intuition and Psychic Sensitivity,* it is important to remember to work your Chakras and wrap your Aura Field daily, for optimum health, balance, and harmony in your life. Develop the habit of *Morning Meditation* and *Nightly Review;* in the morning meditate and work your chakras; in the evening, reflect on your day, journal, and jot down your accomplishments as well as anything you may need to straighten out. Remember, you have twenty-four hours to make amends.

Please try to meditate everyday as you commit to your Spiritual advancement. That never changes!

NOTES

CHAPTER TWO

The Ten Commitments

It is possible to achieve the things you are dreaming about today. With the right intention, focus and perseverance, you will manage to achieve your goal.

The Power of Healing and Transformation is the ultimate reality and shaper of the Universe. This transformative power, which is energetic, unifies all beings as One; a Spiritually-alive, mutually inter-dependent, awesome, marvelous, and magical totality.   —*eaj*

Just about everyone I speak with has a dream they want to pursue. Those same people also have trouble finding the time to make a start on it. "I'm too busy," – that's what they tell me; or, "I don't have time to pursue my dream. I can't fit it in."

I completely understand because my life is busy too. In fact, as I write it's midnight, I could be sleeping, but instead I'm writing this book, completing my three-book trilogy on developing your intuition, and pursuing my intention. I have an underlying belief that if a dream is worth pursuing, then it's worth *making* time for. All it takes is commitment!

There are degrees of commitment. One person may be committed to a project as long as it does not take too much time or energy, while another person may be committed to the same project at the expense of worldly fame and possessions.

The fact is, we cannot make the greatest commitment to everything. It is impossible to make each aspect of life our number one priority. Therefore, we must predetermine the degree of commitment we have toward any one thing.

Paradidomi is translated "committed" in 1 Peter 2:23 (KJV). It literally means, "I give." A personal commitment is to give yourself to the person or thing under consideration.

The word commit comes from the Latin word *committere*, which means to connect, entrust. When we stand behind our words, we demonstrate commitment. Commitment exists when our actions meet the expectation of our words; when there's a congruency between intent, words and action.

Some have said, "The road to hell is paved with "good intentions." People get frustrated, discouraged, fed with negativity, and give up on the intention. They abandon their good. Believe me, I have heard every excuse in the book as to why something has not been accomplished. Just as we think and create the intention, we also create the failure to complete it, through our conscious and subconscious decisions.

Without the power of decision, which includes *being responsible for the effects of our decisions,* we would virtually cease to exist. We are even more than the results of our decisions. This power is somehow connected with the essence of our very being, our Soul. Power of decision leads a person to the fear and guilt that causes disease and now we realize that our decisions can lead back to health.

Decision is the key word as to what and who we are. We are decision. Becoming a Soul was a decision. Choosing to come to Earth for this lifetime was a decision, including our parents, primary family, and the area we were born into.

Every action that takes place is preceded by a deciding intelligence of some kind. I am an intelligence who just moved the pen I am writing with because I decided to. A decider may use thought and emotion, but thought and emotion alone does not create motion. It must also have a physical force. Thought and feeling with no inner decision is powerless.

In some way the very power within us that makes decisions is what we are. Let's say you are deciding between bacon and eggs or pancakes for breakfast, and you have an equal desire for both. Allow your power of decision to fluctuate between the two and you will begin to feel that which is the best for you in this moment. This is the power of decision at work.

Assume that we humans are more than the results of our decisions, but *somehow we are decision* or the power of decision itself. If you knew this was a true statement, what would it mean to you?

Decision plus attention or focus equals consciousness; thinking, talking, action. In other words, consciousness is created by putting your attention on a decision that has been made. The power of decision is eternal and when the decision TO BE, or to become, is made then the *Trinity* of Decision-Consciousness-Attention is instantly made manifest. This trinity is to live this one great Life that was given to you by the Divine or God.

The real me is not just the result of my decisions, but I am Decision, which is a reflection of God. The part of me that actually makes a decision is the real me, the Soul me. When I realize this, I am like God in the fact that I can then become what I decide to become. I am a projection of or aspect of the God Source.

Keep in mind that without decision, there can be no such thing as consciousness or even life or motion. Consciousness, life, and motion are created by decision, and by *applying the Power, the energetic force* behind this is the first step to manifesting hat decision.

In truth, your essence is Decision, and as Decision you have created the reality you find yourself in, whether good or bad. (See Chapter VIII) Slavery and victimization are always caused by the illusion that we have little or no control over the reality we are living, and what we see before us. If we believe we have no control, we acquiesce our real power, become subject to the decisions of others, and become like a leaf floating helplessly along a current down the river of other people's decisions.

By allowing your life to be controlled by the decisions of others, you are put in the position of abdicating yourself from personal responsibility while placing all blame on the decision-makers in your life. Hence, you have given your power away. Instead, you should be the main decision-maker in your own life, which then makes you responsible for your reality in the long run. All those who are in the fifth dimension of evolution, and have become the teachers of this race have the realization they are the *Masters of their reality*.

This is why the sacredness of the vote should never be overlooked. This is an important power the people must always possess if the kingdom of God is to be established on the Earth. As for making changes, if people realized the power of decision within them, any national problem could be turned around tomorrow. Even if only twelve people in Oneness used their power of decision to make changes for the good, the power to change can be enormous. I would venture to say there are not too many mortal people on the Earth who function in unity with a realization of their power to change the Earth for good. Some spiritual groups are beginning to do this now. However, the power of decision is indeed a mystery that has not been utilized to the fullest capacity as yet.

How to Become a Spiritual Being

Thoughts are things. Every though we have creates an energy. If we have a negative thought, we have the power to change that thought. Take the time! Mantras and affirmations are very helpful here. (See: *You Can Heal Your Life* by Louise Hay)

We are in the midst of a transition in the twenty-first century, and it is not easy. Everything is changing, and very quickly. For some people the transition will happen fast, perhaps within a few weeks or months. For others it will take longer.

The environment and our living conditions will change as well. The more other people start to change around you, and grow into the knowledge of Oneness, the easier it will become for you. The energy is set so that everyone who tries will benefit. This is why we have classes and seminars, such as *A Course In Miracles*.

The more you sit, meditate, and absorb the new energies, the clearer you will become. It may be wise to work with a good energetic healer. If you work at this, it will happen, eventually. This energy works like a magnet. We actualize what we visualize, so if you are not happy with your life, change the picture.

You will find that you like everything around you when you become a Spiritual being. It really does not matter what life dishes out to you, because you will eat it with great relish and deep gratitude. As you experience your life, you can enjoy it.

If you give your attention to who you really are, your Soul self, that is what you will become—*Ascended*. Jump off the train or merry-go-round of life. The balance to be achieved is complicated and may take some special healing work on your part. The bottom line is that balance comes, and all will be balanced out evenly and fairly in one way or another.

Here are some good commitments you can make to yourself.

1. Commit to your inner connection with the Divine
2. Commit to raising your consciousness
3. Commit to creating new ways to generate positive energy
4. Commit to persistence – know what you believe and WHY
5. Commit to self-expression and purpose.

6. Pursue your dreams and find your place with the choices you make
7. Use your Vision to bring forth your commitment—believe you are that, in more ways that one
8. Commit to being and doing your best and nurture your Self
9. Commit to positive communication and know that your mind is the lifeblood of your future
10. View confusion at a stepping stone to clarity and believe that you are always more
11. Commit to surrender—create what you desire, live it, and surrender to your commitment.

Making a commitment is similar *to "setting a condition,"* a very important tool for healing and manifesting, which is explained in Chapter X.

NOTES

NOTES

CHAPTER THREE

Frequency Changes—Spontaneous Healing

THE SCIENCE OF THE SOUL

The Soul: the container of the essence of a person's nature and the vehicle for the eternal self. An entity without material reality, regarded as the Spiritual part of a person.   —Websters

Semyon Kirlian, founder of Kirlian photography, discovered a type of energy structure infusing and surrounding the body of all living things in 1939 in Russia, after noticing its appearance around patients while undergoing electro-therapy. Kirlian and his wife then spent the next twenty-five years developing the technology with which to study this energy structure. Using Kirlian technology, biophysicists and biochemists were then able to study this energy structure using an electron microscope. In 1968 scientists in Russia officially announced the discovery of a new energy system in all living things. Biochemists say that this energy body is, *'some sort of elementary plasma-like constellation made of ionized particles, not a chaotic system, but a whole unified organism in itself.'* The scientists studying this energy body called it *'bio-plasma energy'*.

It was further discovered, under closer examination, that this bio-plasma body had certain points of intense energy that corresponded exactly to the 700 main points of the ancient Chinese acupuncture chart. Due to developments from the Kirlians' bio-plasma technology, electronic aids to accurately mark acupuncture points are being used by medical laboratories around the world to treat patients. This is hard evidence that the existence of the bio-plasma body is real and that it is intimately related to our physical body.

What does this bio-plasma body look like? Every living thing placed in the high-frequency discharge produces these patterns. A whole hand can look like the Milky Way, sparking and twinkling against a glowing background of gold and blue. A freshly picked leaf shines with an internal Light that streams out through its pores in beams that gradually flick out one by one as it dies. Leaves taken from the plants of the same species show similar jeweled patterns, but if one of the plants is diseased, the pattern in its leaf is entirely different. Similarly the pattern produced by the same fingertip changes with the mood and health of the man to whom it belongs.

A pattern can have an intrinsic meaning that is more profound than just its appearance. Kirlian also thought about a deeper meaning attached to the bio-plasmic patterns:

'In living things, we see the signals of the inner state of the organism reflected in the brightness, dimness, and color of the flares. The inner life activities of the human being are written in these "light" hieroglyphs. We've created an apparatus to write the hieroglyphs, but to read them, we're going to need help.'

The discovery of the bio-plasma body was nothing new to mystics and psychics; they had always known of its existence and some can even see these patterns and colors. They call it the aura.

Cambridge biologist Oscar Bagnell designed special hollow lenses filled with colored dye that sensitized his eyes and enabled him to view the aura first hand. His description of the human aura is like those describing the bio-plasma body seen using the Kirlian technology. Bagnell describes the aura as being composed of a hazy outer layer and a brighter inner layer, in which there seems to be striations running out at right angles from the skin. Bagnell and other aura watchers say that every once in a while a much brighter *ray "reaches out from the aura like a searchlight"* and extends several feet from the body before vanishing again.'

The bio-plasma body has been observed as a whole unified organism in itself, and just as the human biological organism has a brain and nervous system that produces consciousness, it stands to reason that the bio-plasma organism would have a corresponding structure that would produce consciousness. As its correspondence with acupuncture has shown, the bio-plasma body, or Light body, is connected with, and an extension of, the biological body; and again it stands to reason that there must be something in the bio-plasma body that has to do with the brain and nervous system of the biological body. The bio-plasma body, in short, should contain some extension or alternative plane of consciousness to the brain.

Our physical brains form neuronal patterns from our experience. In a similar way it is likely that our bio-plasma 'brain' would also form patterns from our experience. Biochemists describe the bio-plasma as an organized constellation, so we can see that the concept of pattern-formation fits neatly into the bio-plasma.

The bio-plasma 'brain' is what we call the *Blessed Higher Self*, our *Light Body*, or the *Soul*. Since the physical brain is quite capable of recording our experience and permitting analytical thought, it follows that the Soul would exist for other purposes. Since the Soul must have a purpose, it could be that the Soul records the essence of experience and therefore the essence of personality.

On our journey through life we will go through life-altering and profound realizations. If we think of our own life, and others we know, we may recall the milestones or turning points that have come from the lessons of life. This awareness, or climax points are things a Soul would want to keep on its journey through its many lifetimes. These climaxes are not simply memories (neuronal-brain structures), but are paradigms of consciousness, that is, a new way of seeing, a new way of being, a new plane of awareness, and an evolution of consciousness. A paradigm is a new pattern or model. So we gain a new perceptual and conceptual model to base our experience on, and a new pattern of self is recorded in the bio-plasma as a memory of the Soul. This is known as the *Soul Akashic imprint*.

In times of mystical awareness, transcendent states, or higher consciousness, our consciousness would likely be operating through the Soul. When we elevate our awareness to the Soul vibrationary level, we would experience the *true knowing* of Self (our larger, many lifetimes, ancient Self); hence the phrase from a Gnostic text that says: *you have within you, everlasting life, examine yourself, so you may live.*

If we ascend to our Soul, the Self we realize and become is the Self that never dies, because this is the Self that is reincarnated. The stages, or levels of growth, achieved toward our power of full awareness (our evolving Soul) would need to be 'saved' through reincarnation. In our lifetimes we would always partly be living through our Soul, so a part of us would never die, but our destiny would be to become, as much as possible, our eternal Self. This is known as *Self-realization*, or living in the *State of Being*.

THE SPIRITUAL CHAKRAS
(From: *Ascension—Accessing The Fifth Dimension WORKBOOK*)

In addition to the normal Chakra Energy System there exists an extended chakra system, the *Spiritual Chakras*, which is just now coming into humanity's awareness. This energy system is latent in most people; however, as more people advance Spiritually and begin to Ascend and raise their vibrations, this extended energy system begins to unlock the golden door. This new system, a natural part of the Fifth Dimension, is the next step in the Spiritual evolution of the planet.

In ancient times, the great Masters of Atlantis, as well as many other teachers along the way, were accessing this powerful energy system. In the past, the Fifth Dimension energies have not been available to all, but only to the chosen few. Now, the time has arrived for others to become aware of this system and reap the rewards of using it in their daily and Spiritual lives.

The present understanding of the *chakra system* gives you seven plus one, foot to crown. The extra chakra, Chakra Zero, is your Earth—grounding center and is located at the balls of both feet. Above the Crown Chakra are four more, numbered eight and then ten to twelve. The Ninth Chakra is located at the base of your skull at the back of your head, and the Eight and One—Half Chakra is extended about eight feet out from behind your head, forming a *Triad* between the Eighth and Ninth Chakras.

The main purpose of these extended chakras, which have always been a part of the human energy field, is to enable the individual to tune in to his or her inner God-Self, the Divine Will, and even the galactic community that surrounds and supports the Earth in its evolution. The first Chakra Group, zero to seven, the *Physical Chakras*, are meant to help you with your development regarding the Earth, the Third Dimension; they help you to become One with the planet. Then, the next five chakras, eight to twelve, help you to become *One with the Universe*.

Your awareness is slowly being moved away from your center, your own physical Self, outward to encompass the larger framework of other people, life forces, realities, and divinity itself. In this way, you become more than you were before and more perfect, too. As you stop focusing on yourself and begin to focus on these larger energies, you move out of your small world and step into a new Universe *where almost anything is possible*. From a reality-creating standpoint this movement in possibilities is very, very powerful.

The Advanced Spiritual Chakra System

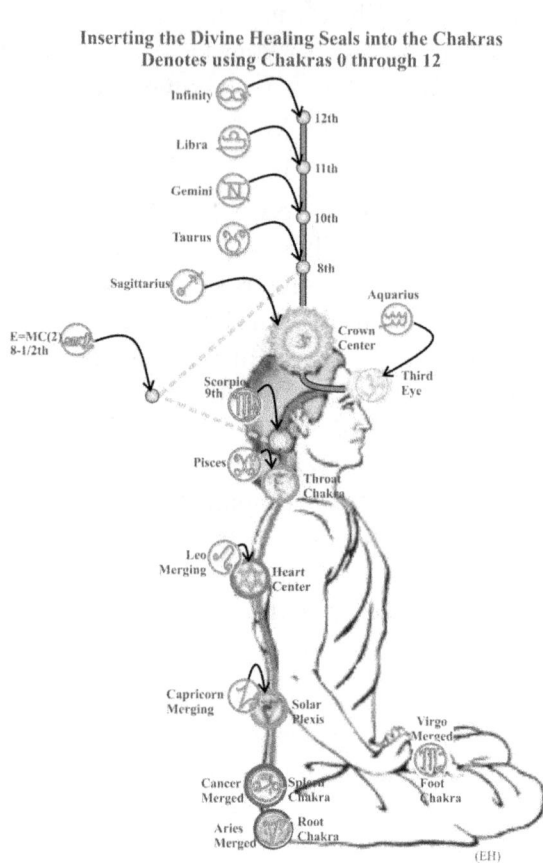

Inserting the Divine Healing Seals into the Chakras
Denotes using Chakras 0 through 12

Infinity

Libra

12th

Gemini

11th

Taurus

10th

Sagittarius

8th

Aquarius

E=MC(2)
8-1/2th

Crown
Center

Scorpio
9th

Third
Eye

Pisces

Throat
Chakra

Leo
Merging

Heart
Center

Capricorn
Merging

Solar
Plexis

Virgo
Merged

Cancer
Merged

Spleen
Chakra

Foot
Chakra

Aries
Merged

Root
Chakra

(EH)

OPENING THE TWELVE CHAKRAS — A SIDE VIEW

This extended Chakra System aids you in the breaking down of the Self within the confines of time and space. To move outward into other dimensions and realities is to come face to face with the idea that the physical Earth is just one place of many that you could have or can inhabit. In the vast regions of the Universe, you have existences that are just as rooted and meaningful as your present earthbound cohabitation is. There are things that you do in these other realities, just like you do here on Earth, and these things are just as significant as your physical lives

Furthermore, when you begin to glimpse these other realities and see what is happening, a new picture of what is developing begins to take shape. You realize that all your existences are like individual musical instruments in a great orchestra that you are directing and creating. You see yourself as a being that transcends time and the physical body.

Each Spiritual Chakra, besides aiding in your own energy development and wellbeing, helps you to touch a particular portion of this vast Universe. *Each Spiritual Chakra opens up a corresponding doorway to another portion of the great vastness that is "The Creator".* During the process you could become aware of past-lives and places that you may begin to access and identify with. You may also begin to remember and utilize talents from the past, and incorporate that learning into your present life.

NOTES

CHAPTER FOUR

Finding Your Angels

We are headed towards an undisputable destiny. The prophecies will be carried out to the letter. Angels will join our two guides, our inner divine helper, uniting with our Blessed Higher Self to deliver new messages, directions, and knowledge.

eaj — 1/7/11

The Angelic Realms from the Seventh Dimension are descending to Earth to give us a helping hand. They are now arriving into the realms of the lower Fifth Dimension—in order to teach. Those that can see and vibrate to this level will be given knowledge—for the first time ever—by the Angels.

All of us have a need to share how the angels have touched us, spoken to us, taught us, or inspired us.

Angel Affirmation: *Angels carry the love of God where he wants it this day. Angels can help you value your desires, and give you an open heart. Cherish these gifts and respect your own sacred feelings.* EAJ

Angels can help you to accept your feelings, open your heart and feel safe, when you express yourself and your innermost feelings. Accept love offered you with gratitude and share yourself with your beloved. You are both made whole by the beauty of love.

As people become increasingly aware of angels, they will experience the joy and delight of angelic contact. Some people who have never actually seen through the veil, will begin to do so as the energetic blocks between our world and theirs becomes thinner. You do not need to be clairvoyant or psychic to see or feel an angel; but you are nevertheless aware of your angel's presence.

It's almost more important to state what angels are not—they are not the Spirits of people who have died. Many know that Angels do exist, and that they are around us all the time.

At the time of one's passing, they come to help us cross over to the other side. They are sent here by a loving God, as a wonderful, unmistakable proof of the love and eternal guidance streaming down from the Divine for each and every one of us.

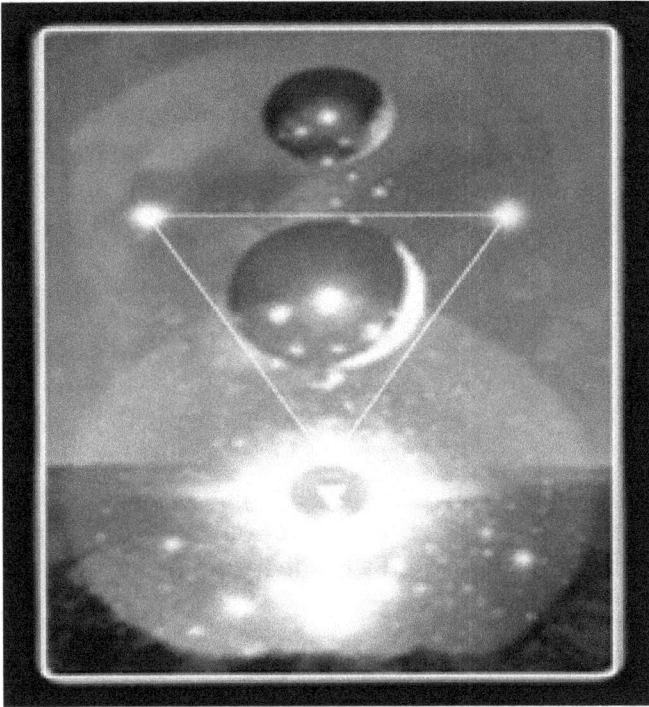

THE NEW ANGELIC ENERGY
DESCENDING INTO US

Angels are *pure spirits* and don't have corporeal forms. They remain disembodied forever. Traditional Catholicism teaches that angels speak "within" a person, and not "to" them, thereby maintaining their spiritual nature.

He has charged His Angels with the ministry of watching and safeguarding every one of His creatures that behold not His face. Kingdoms (Dimensions) have their Angels assigned to them, and men have their Angels; it is the latter to whom religion designates the *Holy Guardian Angels.* Our Lord says in the Gospel, *"Beware lest ye scandalize any of these little ones, for their Angels in heaven see the face of My Father."* The existence of Guardian Angels is real and requires our respect be for this Divine sure and holy intelligence that is ever present at our side; and how great our solicitude be, lest, by any act of ours, we offend those beings, which are ever bent and focused upon us in all our ways!

THE NEED FOR ANGELS

Angels offer unconditional love - they set no rules, no standards to be fulfilled. Angels are here for us this instant, loving and guiding, giving us the support we need to move onwards and upwards towards Spiritual enlightenment.

Angels are beings of Light, and their messages glow with God's energy. Sometimes they don't even have to say anything, but their presence alone communicates clearly the love and protection of God.

Angels will protect us from ourselves as we need and request. When we take the time to meditate and pray, and ask for guidance and support, the desire or request is always received.

To achieve Angelic consciousness is to have the awareness that you are a Divine being, and that you are guided by a higher wisdom in the Universe that operates for your greatest good. There are many levels and dimensions within the Universe. You can provide protection and wisdom to those you love who are at a lower dimension, yet need the guidance of Angels. Much of this is achieved when practicing any type of energy healing. The people who receive your Angel Prayer will feel it on a deep level. They will know of and appreciate your thoughts. Perhaps then you will hear and enjoy the music of the spheres.

Your Spiritual helpers and Angels are there to support you in your relationships with other people. You come into this planet alone and you leave alone, but you can have tremendous communication with others throughout your life. *Praying for abundance and wealth of happiness is not the same as praying to be rich or wealthy.* Just know that you are a child of God and all your needs will be met on a daily basis, and all will be well in your world.

At times, have you become amused as to why you're talking out loud to yourself? What about when, for no apparent reason, you get the "chills" or "goose bumps" on your physical body?

Have you ever felt as if someone was watching out for you? Or wondered if there's more to life after death?

Every religion or philosophy talks about Angels one way or another — and there are many different names for them. These spiritual guides exist in order to help and guide everyone. They come to help us deliver and live out our own unique spiritual message. Angels do without doing. They come for service, to protect us, to warn us, to overshadow us, to deliver a Divine message, as well as to prepare us for Ascension at the end of our physical life.

THE ANGELIC REALM

ST. MICHAEL AND
HIS LEGIONS OF ANGELS

There are different types of angels depicted in the bible that have varying degrees of Divine missions, different names and descriptions. First of all, they are said to be *Messengers of God*. Chreubim, Seraphim, and Arcangels.

IT IS PROPHESIED THAT:
*For the Lord himself shall descend from heaven with a shout, with the voice of the **Archangel** and with the triumph of God; and the dead in Christ shall rise first.* (1 Thess. 4:16)

As a messenger Angel, 'specific Angels' are sent in the form of communicating to people about their personal problems or life decisions. Some believe that the Angel Gabriel submits prayers to heaven (from the 7th Dimension up to the 12th Dimension) or higher, and brings information to us.

Archangel Ariel *is often associated with lions, representing Strength and healing*. When Ariel is near you, you may begin seeing references to or visions of lions around you. Ariel is also associated with the wind. Found in books of Judaic mysticism and Cabalistic, Ariel works closely with King Solomon in conducting manifestation, spirit releasing, and Divine magic.

Ariel also oversees the sprites, the nature Angels associated with water. Ariel is involved with healing and protecting nature, including animals, fish, and birds. If you find an injured bird or other wild animal that needs healing, call upon Ariel for help. Ariel also works closely with Raphael to heal animals in need.

Although he is described as a member of the Angelic hierarchy, he is also at times placed among the evil Angels as one of the fallen Angels who are routed by the stern and obedient seraph Abdiel during the war in heaven. (That is incorrect as he is a true Archangel of God.)

Ariel—"Lion of God".

Archangel Azrael *is the much feared Angel of death* in both Islamic and Hebrew lore, Azrael's name means "whom God helps." Azrael's primary role is to help people cross over to Heaven at the time of physical death. He comforts people prior to their physical passing, makes sure they don't suffer during death and helps them assimilate on the other side. Working as a grief counselor, he surrounds grieving family members with healing energy and helps them cope and thrive, and absorbs their pain.

Azrael has eyes and tongues exactly equal to the number of people inhabiting the world. Each time he blinks one of his eyes, it signifies that another person has died. Azrael also keeps track of the dying by recording the births of the living and erasing the names of those who have died.

Azrael — "Whom God helps".

Archangel Chamuel *is the Archangel of pure love.* Chamuel can lift you from the depths of sorrow and find love in your heart. Chamuel helps us to renew and improve existing relationships as well as finding our Soulmates. (See: Chapter IX) He works with us to build strong foundations for our relationships (as well as careers) so they're long-lasting, meaningful, and healthy. You'll know he's with you when you feel butterflies in your stomach and a pleasant tingling in your body.

If there's a breakdown of your relationship, if you cling to your relationships and don't allow your companion the freedom to be able to express yourself freely, call on Chamuel for guidance and support. The other areas where Chamuel can help is if you need to strengthen a parent-child bond, if you're unable to feel love for yourself or others, if your heart has hardened and is full of negative emotions, if you have lost someone close through death or separation, if you and your children have experienced a divorce, if your heart is blocked with depression, hopelessness and despair, if you feel lonely and broken hearted, if you need to be loved, if you are judgmental and cynical or if you don't appreciate the love that you have in your life.

Chamuel can also help with world peace, career, life purpose and finding lost items.

Chamuel — "He who sees God", "He who seeks God".

Archangel Gabriel is *the Angel of Enunciation* in Daniel. (8:5-26 and 9:21-27). Gabriel also appears in Luke 1-11; *Zechariah was in the sanctuary when an Angel of the Lord appeared, standing to the right of the incense altar. Then the Angel said, "I am Gabriel! I stand in the very presence of God. It was He who sent me to bring you this good news!*

The only Archangel depicted as female in art and literature, Gabriel is known as the "messenger" Angel and is one of the four Archangels named in Hebrew tradition and is considered one of the two highest-ranking Angels in Judeo-Christian and Islamic religious lore. Apart from Michael, she is the only Angel mentioned by name in the Old Testament. She is a powerful and strong Archangel, and those who call upon her will find themselves pushed into action that leads to beneficial results.

Gabriel can bring messages to you just as she did to Elizabeth and Mary of the impending births of their sons, John the Baptist and Jesus of Nazareth. If you are considering starting a family, Gabriel helps hopeful parents with conception or through the process of adopting a child.

Contact Gabriel if your third eye is closed and your Spiritual vision is therefore blocked. If you wish to receive visions of Angelic guidance regarding the direction you are going in. If you wish to receive prophecies of the changes ahead; if you need help in interpreting your dreams and visions.

Gabriel helps anyone whose life purpose involves the arts or communication. She acts as a coach, inspiring and motivating artists, journalist and communicators and helping them to overcome fear and procrastination.

Gabriel also helps us to find our true calling. Ask for Gabriel's guidance if you have strayed from your Soul's pathway, if you wish to understand your life plan and purpose. She can also help if you can find no reason for being or if changes are ahead and you need guidance. If you are contemplating a house move, major purchase or thinking of changing careers.

Call Gabriel if your body is full of toxins and needs purifying and if your thoughts are impure or negative and need clearing and cleansing. Gabriel is also very helpful for women who have been raped or sexually assaulted and feel dirty as well as being under psychic attack, or if you feel that you have absorbed someone else's problems.

Gabriel— "Strength of God"; "The Divine is my strength"; "God is my strength".

Archangel Jeremiel in ancient Judaic texts, is listed as *one of the seven core Archangels*. He is credited with helping Baruch, a prolific author of apocryphal Judaic texts in the first century A.D., with his prophetic visions. It is also said that he took Baruch on a tour of the different levels of Heaven. The coming of the Messiah was one of Jeremiel's visions.

Jeremiel is the Angel who review's our lives with us after we've crossed over. He is the keeper of the Akashic Records. (See Chapter VIII) He is also able to do this for us while we're still living, helping us to review our life up till now so we can correct the wrongs we've done by making positive adjustments. Through this, he's able to help us make life changes, making us stronger and lead us to the right path. Jeremiel also helps us with clairvoyance and prophetic visions, and helps us to interpret psychic dreams.

Jeremiel—("Mercy of God" or "whom God sets up".

Archangel Jophiel *was the Angel present in the Garden of Eden and later watched over Noah's sons*. The Archangel of art and beauty, he is the patron of artists, helping with artistic projects, thinking beautiful thoughts, to see and appreciate beauty around us. Helping to create beauty at home and at work, Jophiel is the Archangel for interior decorators. He illuminates our creative spark by giving us ideas and energy to carry out artistic ventures. He also helps us to see the beauty in all things, including people.

As well as helping our creativity, Jophiel helps us to slow down and smell the roses. Call on him if you need joy and laughter in your life or if you feel you've lost the light in your life. He will also help if your soul is sleeping and needs awakening and if you wish to awaken a deeper understanding of who you are and seeking a connection with the higher self, so that you may take your first steps along your spiritual pathway.

You know Jophiel is at work if you are searching for answers to the questions in your life and wish the greater wisdom to be revealed to you, and all of a sudden you experience flashes of insight in which everything suddenly becomes clear.

Jophiel— "Beauty of God".

Metatron—it is important to note that Metatron is NOT an Angel or Archangel. He was a high guide—and NEVER Enoch reincarnated. This recent teaching is false.

Michael, the Archangel *The first Angel created by God, Michael is the leader of all the Archangels and is in charge of protection, courage, strength, truth and integrity.* Michael appears as a warrior angel, with legions of Angels under his command, (in 1 Thes. 4:16 and Jude 9). Michael is said to be *the Defender Angel who goes to battle.* (Daniel 10:13, 21; and 12:1. Also in Romans 8:38, Eph 1:21 and Col 1:16) *The Angel Michael can order disease* *to leave your body and clear you, aligning you with the Heavenly Realms so that you can strengthen your body and heal.*

Michael is in charge of protection, courage, strength, truth and integrity. Michael protects us physically, emotionally and psychically. He also oversees the Lightworker's life purpose. His chief function is to rid the Earth and its inhabitants of the toxins associated with fear. Michael carries a flaming sword that he uses to cut through etheric cords and protects us from Satan and negative entities. When he's around you may see sparkles or flashes of bright blue or purple light. Call on Michael if you find yourself under psychic attack or if you feel you lack commitment, motivation and dedication to your beliefs, courage, direction, energy, vitality, self-esteem, worthiness. Michael helps us to realize our life's purpose and he's invaluable to Lightworkers helping with protection, space clearing and spirit releasing.

Michael conquered the fallen Angel Lucifer (Satan), was in the Garden of Eden to teach Adam how to farm and care for his family, spoke to Moses on Mount Sinai and in 1950 he was canonized as Saint Michael, "the patron of Police Officers," because he helps with heroic deeds and bravery. Michael also has an incredible knack for fixing electrical and mechanical devices, including computers and automobiles. If your automobile breaks down, call on Michael.

Michael helps us to follow our truth without compromising our integrity and helps us to find our true natures and to be faithful to who we really are. Other times when you may find Michael helpful is when your job is too demanding with impossible deadlines to reach, when you have an addiction, if you're very ill and suffering from a degenerative disease or terminal illness and when you suffer from nightmares.

Michael — "Who is like God", "Like unto God", "Who is like the Divine".

Archangel Raguel is referred to as the *Archangel of Justice and Fairness,* Raguel, just under Archangel Michael, oversees all the other Archangels and Angels. He watches over them to make sure they're working well together in a harmonious and orderly fashion according to Divine order and will.

Raguel is also called the *Archangel for the underdog.* Call on him for help when you need to be empowered and respected. He helps to resolve arguments, helps with cooperation that leads to harmony in groups and families. Raguel defends the unfairly treated, and provides support with mediation of disputes.

In the Revelation of John, Raguel is referred to as an assistant to God in the following account: "*Then shall He send the Angel Raguel, saying: Go and sound the trumpet for the Angels of cold and snow and ice, and bring together every kind of wrath upon them that stand on the left.*"

Despite his exalted position, for some unexplained reason Raguel was reprobated in

745 A.D. by the Roman Catholic church (along with some other high-level Angels, including Uriel). In this day Pope Zachary described Raguel as a demon who "passed himself off as a saint". In Tuuth, Raguel was only following the *Will of God*.

Raguel— "Friend of God".

Archangel Raphael is *the Healing Angel*. Hebrew word rapha means "doctor" or "healer". Raphael is a powerful healer and assists with all forms of healing—humans and animals. Many nurses and physicians claim this angel has guided them; this Angel is ordered into work and heal by Michael.

He helps to rapidly heal body, mind and spirit if called upon, as in the biblical story of Abraham and the pain he felt after being circumcised as an adult. You may call upon Raphael in behalf of someone else, but he can't interfere with that person's free will. If they refuse spiritual treatment, it can't be forced. The chummiest and funniest of all Angels, Raphael is often pictured chatting merrily with mortal beings. He's very sweet, loving, kind and gentle and you know that he's around when you see sparkles or flashes of green light. Part of Raphael's healing work involves spirit releasing and space clearing. He often works with Michael to exorcise discarnate entities and escort away lower energies from people and places. Other areas Raphael helps with is finding lost pets, reducing and eliminating addictions and cravings, clairvoyance, bringing unity to your life, if you feel out of touch with your spirituality, if you've lost a partner and/or your soul/body doesn't feel "whole".

Raphael— Healing power of God", "The Divine has healed", "God heals".

Archangel Raziel works very closely with the Creator and its believed he *knows all of the secrets of the Universe and how it operates*. He wrote down all of these secrets in a tome of symbols and Divine magic called *"The Book of the Angel Raziel"*. After Adam and Eve were expelled from Eden, Raziel gave Adam the book for guidance about manifestation and God's grace. Later the prophet Enoch received the book prior to his ascension and transformation; Noah was also given a copy of the book by Archangel Raphael and Noah used the information to build his ark and help its inhabitants after the flood.

Raziel can help you understand esoteric material, manifestation principles, sacred geometry, quantum physics and other high-level information. He can also open you up to higher levels of psychic abilities and increase your ability to see, hear, know and feel Divine guidance. Like a Divine wizard, Raziel can also assist you with alchemy, clairvoyance, and mystical magic.

Raziel—"God's wisdom keeper." " God's knower".

Archgangel Sandalphon is the only Archangel whose name doesn't end with an "el". *God gave*

Sandalphon his immortal assignment, allowing men in the transformation process to continue their sacred service from Heaven.

Elijah's ascension occurred when he was lifted up to Heaven in a fiery chariot pulled by two horses of fire, accompanied by a whirlwind, an even recorded in the second chapter of the Book of 2 Kings. Elijah continues his sacred assignments from just beneath the Angelic Realm of the Seventh Dimension. (He works in the high part of the Fifth/Sixth Dimension.)

Sandalphon's chief role is to carry human prayers to God so they may be answered. He's said to be so tall that he extends from Earth to Heaven. Ancient Cabalistic lore says that Sandalphon can help expectant parents determine the gender of their forthcoming child and many also believe that he's involved with music as well.

Sandalphon—"God's Heavenly Choir" "God's answer to prayers".

Archangel-The Gatekeeper or **Grim Reaper** is another angel *that appears when a person is dying*. He comes to gently lead them to their spiritual realm. This Angel knows exactly what level, in what dimension, the Soul needs to be placed after death.

Archangel Uriel is *an Angel of Death who is also thought to be the Angel of Transformation,* and is believed to be standing by people on the verge of death.

Uriel is considered one of the wisest Archangels because of his intellectual information, practical solutions, and creative insight, but he is very subtle. You may not even realize he has answered your prayer until you've suddenly come up with a brilliant new idea.

Uriel warned Noah of the impending flood, helped the prophet Ezra to interpret mystical predictions about the coming Messiah and delivered the Cabal to humankind. He also brought the knowledge and practice of *alchemy* and the ability to manifest from thin air, as well as illuminates situations and gives prophetic information and warnings. All this considered, Uriel's area of expertise is divine magic, problem solving, spiritual understanding, studies, alchemy, weather, Earth changes and writing. Considered to be the Archangel who helps with earthquakes, floods, fires, hurricanes, tornadoes, natural disaster and Earth changes, call on Uriel to avert such events or to heal and recover in their aftermath

In the eighth century, the Christian Church became alarmed at the rampant and excessive zeal with which many of the faithful were revering Angels. For some unknown reason, in 145 A.D. under Pope Zachary, a Roman council ordered seven Angels removed from the ranks of the Church's recognized Angels, one of them being Uriel.

Uriel—"God is light", "God's light", "Fire of God".

Angel Moroni — Joseph Smith said that when he was seventeen years of age an angel of God named Moroni appeared to him and said that a collection of ancient writings, engraved on golden plates by ancient prophets, was buried in a nearby hill in Wayne County, New York. The writings were said to describe a people whom God had led from Jerusalem to the Western Hemisphere 600 years before Jesus' birth. According to the narrative, Moroni was the last prophet among these people and had buried the record, which God had promised to bring forth in the latter days. Smith stated that he was instructed by Moroni to meet at the hill annually each September 22 to receive further instructions and that four years after the initial visit, in 1827, he was allowed to take the plates and was directed to translate them into English.

The Angel "Moroni," is based on both prior and later publications, most Latter Day Saints view Smith's 1838 identification of the angel as Nephi as a mistake, perhaps on the part of the transcriber or a later editor. In the version of Smith's 1838 history published by *The Church of Jesus Christ of Latter-day Saints,* as well as the portion canonized by that denomination as the Pearl of Great Price, the name "Nephi" has been changed by editors to read "Moroni". The Community of Christ publishes the original story, including the identification of "Nephi", but indicates "Moroni" in a footnote.

In addition to Joseph Smith, several other early Mormons said they had visions where they saw the angel Moroni. According to the Book of Mormon, Moroni was the son of Mormon, the prophet for whom the *Book of Mormon* is ostensibly named. Because of his instrumentality in the restoration of the gospel, Moroni is commonly identified by Latter-day Saints as the angel mentioned in Revelation 14:6, *"having the everlasting gospel to preach unto them that dwell on the earth, and to every nation, and kindred, and tongue, and people."*

It is also said that Moroni led a mortal life, and thus cannot be considered as a part of the Angelic Realms of the Seventh Dimension, as no Angel has even been in human form. Moroni works in the same realm as Elija.

Angel/Master Teacher Maroni - Joseph Smith

Your Personal Guardian Angel, who dwells at the gate of your Soul School, where the Soul ascends after death, is an aspect of Michael. All personal guardian angels, as well as those who protect nations, are a part of St. Michael's *Legions of Angels*. The Earth is also provided with an Angel, which is another aspect of St. Michael.

The meaning of Angels throughout history across the world are said to have different powers, and can help or give aid to their followers or believers. Each Angel has a distinct purpose and name, and is a part of Archangel Michael and his *Legion of Angels*. In medieval times it was thought that Angels were humans with higher powers, endowed with an intelligence, voice, and free will, that humans could never hope to attain. Therefore some of these beings could practice witchcraft and evil doings. This is not true. What those beings were, are called Druids.

The Legions of Angels are not Archangels. The truth is Angels have many shapes, forms, sizes, appearances, and duties. You will see Angels as you need to see them. Sometimes you may see only a burst of Light in a darkened room or a Light Form around a person's body.

The following story is a true encounter with Angels, and was written by my mother when my sisters were about four years old. My twin and I weren't even thought about yet.

An Angel's Miracle

Nancy was a beautiful and healthy identical twin girl, four years old. She and her twin were bright spots in our life the year of 1941. In April, Nancy suddenly developed some health problems and was eventually diagnosed with spinal meningitis. We rushed her to the hospital in the middle of the night just before Holy Week.

At the hospital she cried continually because she was in such pain and could not sit up. Spinal meningitis is a highly communicable disease, and Nancy had to be isolated. We could only visit with her by wearing masks, white coats, and looked at her through a glass window.

We spent most of Holy Thursday, 1941, at Hackensack Medical Center in New Jersey, where she was treated.

Nancy's twin, Claramay, became our link to hope. Claramay was positive that Nancy would live. She claimed that her twin would never leave her. Although Claramay was not allowed near the hospital, every morning she would tell us that Nancy was coming home soon.

"An angel came to me in a dream and asked me if I wanted my sister to leave. I stomped my foot and clenched my fists and said no! Then the angel nodded her head, smiled, and faded away. My sister is coming home."

"Claramay is praying for me," Nancy would say. My husband and I had always trusted in God in our own way, but little Claramay believed with her whole being.

Nancy seemed to be holding her own for awhile; then one night, two weeks after the onset of the disease, she became much worse. Her head was bent backwards and she looked as if she were doing a back bend. She could not breathe well, and the pain was unbearable. Finally the doctor told us that she might not make it through the night.

This was no time for tentative prayers. My husband and I cried out from deep within our Souls, "God, send your merciful angel to heal our daughter!"

Within minutes Nancy suddenly sat up straight in her hospital bed. "Mama look.," she cried and was smiling, "Mama, Daddy, look!"

Nancy was pointing to the ceiling over her bed. She folded her arms across her chest and wriggled her fingers on her shoulders, pretending to have wings. Then she laughed out loud while spreading out her arms and pretending to fly.

"It's an angel," she explained. "The angel came to heal me. She told me my twin sister sent her."

We were shocked and tongue-tied. A nurse came rushing into the room, and when she saw Nancy sitting up and smiling, she stopped short in her tracks.

"Oh my goodness, she exclaimed, "It's as if she's been risen up for Easter." Upon examination, Nancy's fever was gone, and her spine was straight.

When we returned home late that evening, little Claramay came running to the door. The sitter explained to us that she refused to go to bed.

"My sister is coming home. Where is she? She's coming home today. The angel told me so," Claramay shouted excitedly.

Although Nancy had to remain in the hospital for a few more days, she was healed of that fatal disease without disfigurement or paralysis. Upon Nancy's arrival home, the girls hugged each other and huddled together.

"She was beautiful, don't you think?" Claramay asked Nancy.

"Yes, with such pretty golden hair and her long blue dress. The sunlight was glowing around her," Nancy responded. Then they giggled, realizing they had both seen the same vision.

Quietly, I remembered the miracle of Easter. I knew then that something special had happened; something beyond the ordinary. My spine tingled at this awareness. Tears filled my eyes as I gave thanks for my daughter's life.

I was sure my daughter was well and that she would never have such an ordeal to live through again. God had sent down an angel to help my daughter and her twin get though some terrifying days. The Lord had allowed these children to hear His voice, bringing to them assuring words of mercy and healing. All of us knew deep inside that Nancy's life had been saved by the grace of an angel.

—Priscilla Rhoda Hemphill Reich

All of us have a need to share how the angels have touched us, spoken to us, taught us, or inspired us.

What are Fallen Angels?

Fallen Angels are those Angels who rebelled against God and have "fallen" from grace and the presence of God. There are many theories as to how these Angels fell from grace, but there is nothing written as to why this happened, except for a brief passage in Genesis 6, where the sons of God (Angels) "saw the daughter of men... and took them wives". But this explanation was dismissed when it was determined that Angels were androgynous, being neither distinctly male nor female.

The chief of the fallen Angels was Satan, one of God's highest Angels. He led a revolt against God and was banished from heaven, along with his followers, which is said to be a third of all the Angels. Satan was driven from Heaven by the Archangel Michael and the Angels of light, and cast into hell. Other names given Satan have been Prince of Darkness, Lucifer, Beelzebub, Devil, Samael, Mastema, Beliel Duma, Azazel, Mephistopheles, and Iblis.

(To learn more about the Fallen Angels, read *Planet In Rebellion* by George E. Vandeman)

(To create your Angel Altar – *See Opening to Your Intuition and Psychic Sensitivity—Book One* – pg. 144)

NOTES

CHAPTER FIVE

Accessing The New Energies

The Seven Steps to Happiness
By Yogi Bhajan

HAPPINESS
When you do something for someone else,
which seems impossible, and you do it really
well, you feel very elevated. You feel exalted.
That is Happiness.

SACRIFICE

You can stand any pain for that person. That
sacrifice gives you HAPPINESS.

GRACE

Where there is Grace, there is no interference,
no gap between two people. No hidden agenda.
Grace gives you the power to SACRIFICE.

DIVINITY

Divinity is when people have no duality about
who you are. They trust you at first sight. They
have no fear of you. Divinity give you GRACE.

DIGNITY

People start trusting you, liking you and
respecting you. Dignity will give you
DIGNITY.

CHARACTER

Character is when all your characteristics - all
facets, flaws, and facts - are under your control.
Your personal response system. Yin and Yang
meet, are centered, and totally balanced.
Character is what you take with you at Death,
and developing your character gives you
DIGNITY.

COMMITMENT

The first step is Commitment - and Setting
Conditions for your life path. In every life you
have to commit. That is why the word is
commit-meant.
Commitment gives you CHARACTER.

The Ascension to the Fifth Dimension has already begun. We have witnessed miracles that have changed what we believe as we vibrated through the Fourth Dimension. These prior miracles have opened a doorway to powerful new ways, bringing us a new consciousness as the world knowledge and science are changed.

WORKING WITH THE TWO BODIES

We have our *physical body* that we live through, and which we are very familiar with. However, seventy percent of our being is invisible, and carries within it our other half, or *Spiritual (Universal) body* as well. Within this etheric, Universal body, are the new Spiritual Chakras, and a new energy to open them and access the new spiritual powers. (See *Ascension—Accessing the Fifth Dimension-WORKBOOK—Chakras Chart*)

We have learned that miracles are possible beyond the limits of the laws of science, bringing peace, healing, abundance, and change. The shift described by the ancients as well as many in this day and time will take us beyond the limits of our past.

The four dimensions have come together, creating a *vortex*. As the four energies come together, they create a circle, now known as the *Circle of Light*, that is the power point entrance into the energies of the Fifth Dimension; this vortex is a powerful healing center and leads to all other dimensions. As you are pulled toward and enter the vortex, which penetrates the Fifth Dimension membrane, you are walking into the center of its matrix; a surrounding substance within which something else originates, develops, or is contained; a vibrating membrane that heals, protects, and purifies; this is within the Double Helix of the new system.

Each dimension has its own matrix. By entering the vortex, you have passed through the limiting membrane of the matrix surrounding the Fourth Dimension. There is no choice here, as everything eventually will be pulled into the Fifth Dimension, releasing and eradicating all four prior dimensions.

After moving through the vortex and entering the matrix of the Fifth Dimension, you will begin working with the new *Spiritual matrix*, unique to this dimension. The physical matrix contains the Third Dimension, the primary matrix contains the Fourth Dimension, and the Spiritual matrix, the Fifth.

Unveiling the Spiritual matrix is like peeling off the layers of an onion. As you peel away the layers of unreality, eventually you will locate the *inner being,* or *Spiritual Body.* Though your eyes may tear from time to time, there is a great reward awaiting you at the center of this Double Helix of energy.

This movement caused a process, which began at the new millennium and continues into 2026. Once we become aware of these life-altering discoveries, we will and must think of ourselves differently.

This is your *Soul's growing program* at work. The human being does not automatically grow into his ultimate form. It comes from choices, along with trial and error. With each unveiling, with each layer falling away, a new reality emerges. Every time a new level is reached, the human being must then change and alter his physical reality.

He must stretch beyond the current reality to find and appreciate his own universally created growing pattern and how that pattern is connected to all life. The key to understanding that process is locked within the individual's astrological birth chart. Each individual possesses the freedom to ask and answer the questions: *Who am I? Why am I here? Who is really the I Am?*

These questions help one to begin the search, and this search takes people forward to an automatic realization of their destiny in physical form, to the core of all life, their individual Soul school, and finally, to the eternal center of all life in pursuit of advancing along the Spiritual matrix.

The Spiritual matrix, which is divided into five parts, has other names. It is also called the Soul or "emotional heart" at the Tenth Chakra located in the Fifth Dimension. The Spiritual matrix is the Soul's fully developed growth pattern and potential. This matrix contains within it a connecting link to the life force or Godhead center, which is in the Twelfth Dimension.

This life-sustaining power sent out to this matrix is the basis upon a physical life that is built successfully in the Third Dimension. A Soul determines to begin life on Earth in the physical body in the energies of the Fifth Dimension, such as Indigo children. Attunement with the Spiritual body brings awareness of how to create physical objects and events on Earth such as wellness, happiness, health, finances, romance, your home and lifework, without losing sight of Spiritually evolved values.

Finding ways to develop your own life program, while consistently improving and refining your life experience, is how you find peace and contentment. When you are growing in harmony within your Spiritual matrix, all other purely physical manifestations flow into harmony, and your desires are achieved.

True happiness cannot be achieved through learning only on the physical levels. The Spiritual body must be discovered, experienced, and finally known. As the Solar System and the Earth plane leave the Third Dimension forever, we will learn that the Spiritual and physical rightfully proceed as partners and are expanding into an otherwise limited living experience.

The key to healing and Ascension is to understand what a belief or mind-set is and how setting a condition works beyond these limits. Thousands of people have come to me seeking answers to creating a better life, better health, and more satisfying partnerships, so they can develop and deepen their Spirituality. Many wish to live more constructive and harmonious lives.

That desire is the beginning of climbing to a new Spiritual level. If the pathway to Spiritual levels was easily found or accessed, we would have no need for this Earth school. Most of us are living this illusion known as life, the all encompassing preoccupation with physical existence which takes all of one's waking hours and leaves no time or thought to the more subtle reality which will transcend our physical death.

The Soul comes to Earth to have the opportunity to live through and master the level it is on with a rare opportunity to transcend up to another level or two. If this is not accomplished in the first lifetime, then rebirth is the only way a Soul can move up a notch or two on the Ascension staircase.

Over the past thirty years, as my experience grew and my reality broadened by working closely with my Blessed Higher Self, my perceptions of reality changed dramatically. All of our outer experiences are created from our inner thoughts. This is a difficult concept to grasp. I grew increasingly aware that there was a subtle shift from the three dimensional reality into another life experience, the Fourth Dimension and beyond.

When one walks in the energies of the Fourth Dimension, telepathy kicks in big time, and thoughts form a reality quickly. After realizing this as a true fact and working with the breath classes and kundalini yoga, as taught by Yogi Bhajan, it became a natural phenomenon for me. I could actually breathe away fear, create a void and manifest a desire. It works with body pain as well.

I realized that most of us wish to live more constructive and harmonious lives and began designing classes to guide people into the higher levels. As was always the case, after the intensive weekends or monthly séances, the people who attended moved into a higher level of reality, at least for awhile, and their lives changed dramatically.

The more I developed and expanded these classes, the more aware I became of how the different levels affect us, how we move between them, and how the "real" could become the "unreal" as well as create the desired outcome. This is working in the Fourth Dimension reality.

Dr. Deepak Chopra calls this *"Quantum Physics."* Whoever realized that thoughts are really things? They are a powerful energy we humans inherited at birth, and they can work for us while creating our personal reality.

A personal reality without a Spiritual connection is truly an illusion as well as an empty life. To live within this illusion is painful. The all encompassing preoccupation with physical existence eats up all of our waking hours and leaves a blindness to the reality of wisdom and knowledge that transcends physical death; this is discouraging and depressing at best.

Personal illusion is, in fact, any part of the human belief system that negates a

Spiritual/Universal/Oneness core and interaction with all life. This illusion appears to be real but is, in fact, a sham. It's the great pretender or the weasel as the Native Americans call it.

This illusion can create such a power over us. This higher reality, on the other hand, brings in the authentic, the genuine foundation of unlimited realities and understanding. This planet contains within it the energy level that creates the possibilities to understand motives and actions of others with compassion and a brighter awareness.

The new Fifth Dimension personal reality begins in any phase, within any of the twenty-eight levels, which shows the Soul that man's physical presence is an illusion, a momentary consciousness that can be altered by Light to a far more expansive, prosperous, happy, and balanced form of life.

Louise Hay says *"Change your mind and you will change your reality."*

There can be a starkness, an emptiness, creating a need to find responsibility and reliability from deep within. Then you find your personal reality because this reality is always based on *truth*. It is the barest of facts about who you are, from whence you evolved in past lifetimes, what you came to learn in this lifetime, as well as how your Soul is handling that assignment.

The eternal quest in search of getting closer to God calls out to each Soul to seek beyond your present life illusions, to find the irrefutable, the non-negotiable reality of who you are. This search usually begins when you have completed one stage and are ready for the disillusionment, the jump from a myth or old belief system into a new awareness and reality.

When this illusion is shattered, it begins a chain reaction, breaking one illusion after another until all barriers are destroyed. You step forward whole and complete, transformed, but feeling alone.

This can be a most painful experience. To truly see oneself, one's life, one's environment and belief system in the full White Light of "what is" can be overwhelming. The human body and mind do not easily accept drastic steps and reprogramming.

The new dimension you have entered makes it possible for you to find the reality in all things. As you search this dimension, you discover knowledge and secrets that unfold and become revealed. With each step upward, a new understanding comes, creating more questions, and then the energies bring the answers, giving you greater compassion and understanding of how life works. This Ascension process is a pulling together of new discoveries into a cohesive unit of self-understanding.

Most of these lessons come from the Soul's ethereal body. This body travels up to Universal knowledge or to the Blessed Higher Self and brings back the information to the mind within the physical body. While this searching may take a long time, lifetimes, in fact, there is every reason for you to begin this inward journey immediately.

The essence of life, the path of value and substance, lies in the search and realization of the individual and cosmic reality. They have to coincide and work together at this time, or the life span will dissolve and come to an end.

The "unreal" or Spiritual body/mind/Spirit is always in a state of flux and constantly changing: physically, mentally/emotionally, and spiritually. The real Self or the Universal/ethereal body is the 'bona fide' you.

That is the self that sends out healing energies, receives your Divine messages, brings your gut reactions, and strengthens your intuitive and psychic senses. It is not the physical body that is in touch with God—it's the mind and ethereal energies we all possess.

We are on the threshold of a new time, a new era of enlightenment, peace and calm. Today the Spiritual body holds a much broader vision. *As complete envelopment into the Fifth Dimension arrives, the Spiritual matrix must integrate with the physical body if we are to survive.* This began around December 21, 2012, when the new vibration entered and raised the consciousness of life on this planet. This energetic vibration lasted for seventy-two hours. It is known as creating the zero point.

The physical body and mind merged with the invisible realms of the eternal, while at the same time maintaining an *unalterable course* toward Spiritual enlightenment. Each and every one of us is now walking this new path.

In Atlantis, around 10,000 BC, awareness of and working within the levels of the Spiritual matrix was an everyday occurrence. The Atlanteans lived completely immersed in the Fifth Dimension.

After their extinction and the evolvement of the new human in the Third Dimension, we swung from a state of total interaction to a one of practically nonexistent interaction with our Spiritual matrix. The reawakening began in the 1960's, and the new age search took us into the twenty-first century. The pendulum is again swinging, faster and faster, back toward self-integration of the Spiritual and non-spiritual.

In the past, everyone lived his life in tune with the 'voice' that was heard from within his Spiritual matrix: the voice of his ethereal body, sending messages from the Blessed Higher Self as well as new Universal knowledge. The physical-thinking brain and spiritually intuitive mind functioned as one.

There was not the present day delineation between Divine awareness and the physical life. Man was indeed limited in his conceptual understanding of the world around him, but the thoughts he did have were linked to his total life. When he went hunting, he automatically tuned in and combined the learned fundamentals of hunting with a broader understanding of life as a flowing, ongoing, ever-changing experience.

There was no need to hide behind a façade or separate himself from life around him. He knew he might become food for the animal he hunted, or the animal might become his food. Life existed as an uncomplicated integration of attunement, thinking, and then action.

As man moved along, he felt a need to dissect and explain everything he saw. He drew away from his intuitive God-connection and began to see himself as the center of the Universe. This trend culminated with the Post-Industrial Revolution man, who became completely caught up in the value of his own scientific contributions. His fascination with his human power as well as his physical abilities excluded a belief in a more subtle, veiled, yet all-encompassing force.

He believed in only what he could tangibly touch and interact with. Within his new, illusionary world as inventor, he saw himself alone as pivotal to the progress of civilization and evolution.

This change from the totally intuitive man to the totally self-absorbed man has been the natural development of the human species, but now it is time once again for the integration of both worlds. Physical and Spiritual matrices are not mutually exclusive, as they are each meant to complement the other, bringing man to a place of greater accomplishment and creativity.

On December 21, 2012, a rare celestial alignment culminated, aligning the galactic center and our Solar System. At this point, the Winter Solstice Sun aligned with the center of the Milky Way Galaxy, the home of our Solar

System, together with at least 200 billion other stars, and created a "sky portal" in the "dark rift" of the Milky Way.

The morphogenetic quality began on that date. This era will be known as *"Galactic Synchronization."* A new galactic cycle began in 1999, and we continued to see accelerated changes in predictable directions until 2011, when another new galactic cycle began on February 2, 2011, leading to Universal consciousness and the end of linear history. Take a look at your lives and see how much changed, fell away, and pushed you into a new direction at that time.

We have a lot of inner work to do as we integrate these energies. Man is indeed the creator of his own reality, but not as a separate force. There is too much he cannot discover or begin to understand until he flows with the Universal energy of God. *This is called coming into the Oneness.* He must dispel his own illusion of sole importance in the Universe, drop the ego, and accept the reality of a valid and essential attachment to all life through accessing the Spiritual body and new matrix.

Man is not, and has never been, except by his own choice, rooted to a simple completion of a preordained growth cycle. Instead, he is free to creatively blend the physical and the Spiritual matrices, allowing the body and mind freedom to fulfill their life patterns. This is what defines free will. This is the search for the question we always ask, "Who am I?"

The Lord said, *"I am that I Am." (John 4:26; 6:20; 8:24, 28, 58; 13:19; 18:5)*

The new science, Quantum Physics, is bringing man back to using the intuitive, back to reality. For with every mystery that is explainable there are five which are not. Individuals now feel closer to the vastness, the great majesty of the unexplainable. They are less threatened by the possibility of an emptiness or obliqueness after death. The awesomeness of this unsolved puzzle...*do we have life after death?* is helping the human race suspend the illusion of sole importance in order to recognize the need of joining all the life forces.

The Resurrection is at hand. We are returning to the Atlantean energies, its buried Spiritual matrix, and perhaps beyond that. This is the only true way the individual and collective consciousness has of becoming healed and whole.

If you have any questions about how to begin a Spiritual Practice see Chapter XI,
or send your e-mail to:

Elizabeth.joyce.email@gmail.com

NOTES

CHAPTER SIX

The Advanced Spiritual Chakra System

Inserting the Divine Healing Seals into the Chakras
Denotes using Chakras 0 through 12

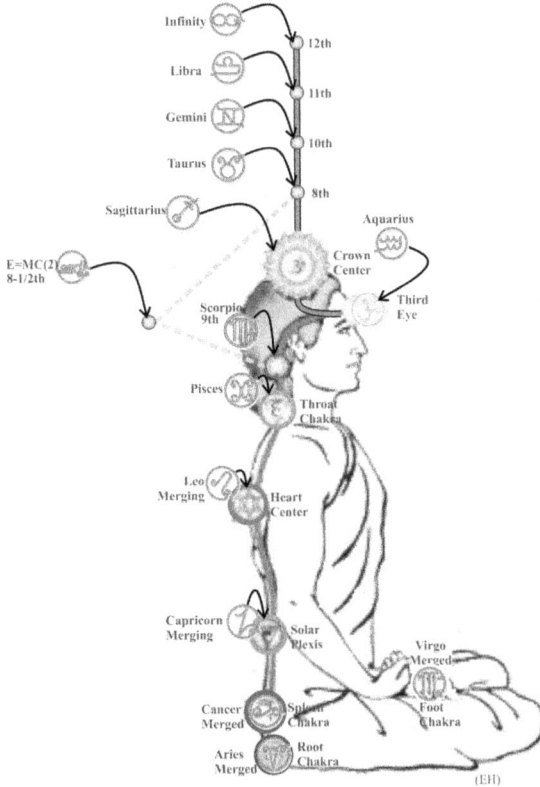

Infinity

Libra

Gemini

Taurus

Sagittarius

E=MC(2)
8-1/2th

12th

11th

10th

8th

Aquarius

Crown
Center

Third
Eye

Scorpio
9th

Pisces

Throat
Chakra

Leo
Merging

Heart
Center

Capricorn
Merging

Solar
Plexis

Virgo
Merged

Cancer
Merged

Spleen
Chakra

Foot
Chakra

Aries
Merged

Root
Chakra

(EH)

Chakra 12 - Connection to the Higher Dimensional level of Divinity, advanced Spiritual skills, Ascension, connection to the Universe and beyond.

Chakra 11 - Pathway to the Soul, the individual's ability to acquire advanced Spiritual skills (travel beyond the limits of time and space, teleportation, bi-location, instantaneous precipitation of thoughts, telekinesis in some cases)

Chakra 10 – The Heart Center of the Spiritual Chakras. Divine creativity, synchronicity of life; the merging of the masculine and feminine within, unlocking of skills and higher energies contained in the Ninth Chakra

Chakra 9 - Soul Blueprint (the individual's total skills and abilities learned in all the life times) Contains all karma, knowledge, and actions since the Soul was created.

Interfacing Chakra (8.5)—Amber/Mother of Pearl   There is a half-spin chakra between the Eighth and the Ninth Chakra, spinning at a lower rate. This chakra brings a clear triad connection between the Third Eye, Ninth Chakra, and the Crown Center, and it governs emotional and mental clarity. Problems with any of these areas usually show up here, and express themselves as a Fifth Dimensional headache. This Chakra vibrates half in the Fourth Dimension and half in the Fifth

Dimension. *It is your bridge to accessing and ascending to the higher levels.*

Chakra 8 - Energy center of Divine Love, Spiritual compassion, and Spiritual selflessness, holds your karmic residue, activates Spiritual skills and purification contained in the Seventh Chakra,

Chakra 7 - Chakra) Traditionally your connection to the Divine (Human level of Divinity), contains programs to be used by 8th and 9th Chakra including the release of basic psychic skills (telepathy, seeing auras, lucid dreaming, out-of-body travel, healing) and feeds this to the 6th Chakra – the Third Eye.

AN OVERVIEW

Opening your Third Eye accelerates your Spiritual growth.

Besides the normal Chakra Energy System there exists an extended chakra system, which is just now coming into humanity's awareness. This energy system is latent in most people; however, as more people advance Spiritually, this extended energy system begins to unlock the Golden Door. This extended Chakra system, a natural part of the Fifth Dimension, is the next step in the Spiritual evolution of the planet.

Once, a long time ago, the Great Masters of Atlantis and our Spiritual Masters along the way were of the few to access and use this powerful energy system. Now, the time has come for others to become aware of this system and reap the rewards of using it in our daily and Spiritual lives.

The present understanding of the chakra system gives you seven plus one (foot to crown). The extra chakra (Chakra Zero) is your Earth-grounding center, and it is located in the balls of your feet. Now, above the Crown Chakra are four more, numbered eight to twelve. The main purpose of these extended chakras, which have always been a part of the human energy field, is to enable the individual to tune in to his or her inner God-Self, the Divine Will, and even the galactic community that surrounds and supports the Earth in its evolution

The first Chakra Group (zero to seven) helps you with your development regarding the Earth, the Third Dimension; they help you to become One with the planet. Then, the next five (eight to twelve) help you to *become One with the Universe*. Your awareness is slowly being moved away from your center, your own physical self, and working outward to encompass the larger framework of other peoples, life forces, realities, and Divinity itself. In this way, you become more than you were before and more perfect, too. As you stop focusing on yourself and begin to focus on these larger, expanded energies, you move out of your small world and step into a new area, the entire Universe, where almost anything is possible. From a reality-creating standpoint, this movement in possibilities is very, very powerful.

One of the things that the extended chakra system aids in is the breakdown of the Self within the confines of time and space. To move outward into other dimensions and realities is to come face to face with the idea that the physical Earth is just one place of many that you could have or can inhabit; other places in the more vast regions of the Universe. You may have existences in other parts of the Universe that are just as rooted as your present earthbound cohabitation.

There are things that you do in these other realities, just like you do here on Earth, and these things are just as significant as your physical lives. Furthermore, when you begin to glimpse these other realities and see what is happening, a new picture of what is developing begins to take shape. You realize that all your existences are like individual musical instruments in a great orchestra that you are directing and creating. You see yourself as a being able to transcend time and the physical body.

Each Spiritual Chakra, besides aiding in your own energy development and wellbeing, helps you to touch a particular portion of this vast Universe. *Each Spiritual Chakra opens up a corresponding doorway to another portion of the great vastness that is "The Creator".* There is a natural order to each chakra in that the opening of one leads very gently to the opening of the next. Because of this ordering, these centers will awaken one by one—as your body allows, with each center becoming more alive as another, higher Spiritual chakra begins to spin in synchronicity with the chakras below it.

There is a pattern to this opening, if you were to observe it from a perspective of time. Generally, the 8th Chakra Center will open first, which remains in your aura field in the Fourth Dimension, with a delay before another expansion occurs. Then, after this process, the 9th will open, hooking you into the new Fifth Dimension energies with the 8.5 Chakra acting as a protective filter, and, once opened, the 10th will show just a glimmer of activity. At this point, the 8th Chakra Center will expand more. Then, when the 10th Center actually starts to open, the 9th Center will experience another expansion with the 8th Center expanding even further.

The next level or octave will have the 11th Chakra Center expanding with the 12th Center showing just a glimmer of activity. Then the process repeats, spinning in harmony with the lower Spiritual Chakras. It's a kind of wave effect, with each center opening up and waving its vibrational energy down into the other centers, enabling them to open up and expand.

Elizabeth Joyce

Ascension Invocation to Unify the Chakras

I breathe in Universal Light
Through the center of my heart,
Opening my Heart Chakra
Into a beautiful ball of Yellow/Gold Light,
Allowing my Blessed Higher Self, my Universal Body,
To expand throughout my Aura.

I breathe in Universal Light
Through the center of my Heart Chakra,
Allowing the Light to expand,
Encompassing my Throat Chakra
And my Solar Plexus Chakra
In one unified field of Light
of Green, Yellow/Gold, and Blue
Within, through, and around my body.
To expand throughout my Aura.

I breathe in Universal Light
Through the center of my Heart Chakra,
Allowing the Light to expand,
Encompassing my Brow Chakra And my Navel Chakra
In one unified field of Light
of Green, Yellow/Gold, Indigo, and Silver
Within, through, and around my body.
To expand throughout my Aura.
Encompassing my Crown Chakra
And my Root Chakra In one unified field of Light
Of Red, Yellow/Gold, and Violet/Silver
Within, through, and around my body.
To expand throughout my Aura.

I breathe in Universal Light
Through the center of my Brow Chakra,
Allowing the Light to expand,
Encompassing my Eighth Chakra
Eight inches above my head
And my Ninth Chakra
Eight inches behind my head
In one unified field of Light
Of Indigo/Silver, Ultra-Violet, and Magenta/Silver
Within, through, and around my body.
I allow a Wave of Highest Consciousness
To move between these three points.
I AM One with Universal Light.

I breathe in Universal Light
Through the center of my Brow Chakra,
Allowing the Light to expand,
Encompassing my Eighth Chakra
(Eight feet above my head)
Around to my upper thighs
In one unified Circle of Light
Of Indigo/Silver, Ultra-Violet, and yellow/Gold
Within, through, and around my body.
I allow my emotional body to merge
With my physical body.
I AM One with Universal Light.

I breathe in Universal Light
Through the center of my heart,
Allowing the Light to expand,
Encompassing my Ninth Chakra
(Eight Feet Behind my head)
And my lower thighs
In one unified Circle of Light
Of Indigo/Sliver, Magenta/Silver, and Yellow/Gold
Within, through, and around my body.

I allow my consciousness
The Universal Body to merge
With my physical body.
I AM One with Universal Light.

I breathe in Universal Light
Through the center of my Brow Chakra,
Allowing the Light to expand,
Encompassing my Tenth Chakra
(Twelve Feet above my head)
Around to my knees
In one unified Circle of Light
Of Indigo/Silver, Ultraviolet, and Clear/Yellow
Within, through, and around my body.
I allow my Spiritual Universal Body and Chakras
To merge with my physical body,
Forming the unified field.

I breathe in Universal Light
Through the center of my Brow Chakra,
Allowing the Light to expand,
Encompassing my Eleventh Chakra
(Twenty-Four Feet above my head)
And my upper calves
In one unified Circle of Light Of Indigo/Silver,
Deep Indigo Silver, and Yellow/Gold
Within, through, and around my body.
I allow the Universal Body to merge
With the unified field.
I AM One with Universal Light.

I breathe in Universal Light
Through the center of my Brow Chakra,
Allowing the Light to expand,
Encompassing my Twelfth Chakra
(Thirty-Six Feet above my head)
And my lower calves
In one unified Circle of Light
Of Indigo/Silver, Diamond/Clear, and Yellow/Gold

Within, through, and around my body.
I allow the Holy and Divine Masters to merge
Within the unified field.
I AM One with Universal Light.

I breathe in Universal Light
Through the center of my Heart Chakra,
Allowing the Light to expand,
Encompassing my Thirteenth Chakra
The Golden Door
(Forty-Four Feet Above my head)
And my Foot Chakras
In one unified Circle of Light
Of Yellow/Gold, Amber, and Diamond/Clear
Within, through, and around my body.
I allow the I AM vibrations to merge
With the unified field.
I AM One with Universal Light.

I breathe in Universal Light
Through the center of my Heart Chakra,
Allowing the Light to expand,
Encompassing my Spiritual and Physical bodies
To below my feet, surrounding my Aura
In one unified Circle of Light Clear/Yellow and Amber
Within, through, and around my body.
Creating the fourth circle around my Aura Field.
I allow the Source's Presence to vibrate and move
Throughout this unified field.
I AM One with Universal Light.

I breathe in Universal Light
Through the center of my Heart Chakra.
I ask that the highest level of my Spirit
To Radiate forth from my center,
The Fourth and 10th Chakras
Filling this unified field completely.
I radiate forth throughout this day.
I AM One with Universal Light.

Within, through, and around my body.
Creating the fourth circle around my Aura Field.
I allow the Source's Presence to vibrate and move
Throughout this unified field.
I AM One with Universal Light.

I breathe in Universal Light
Through the center of my Heart Chakra.
I ask that the highest level of my Spirit
To Radiate forth from my center,
The Fourth and 10th Chakras
Filling this unified field completely.
I radiate forth throughout this day.
I AM One with Universal Light.
I live within the Universal Light.

I love within the Universal Light.
I walk within the Universal Light.
I AM sustained and nourished By the Universal Light.
I joyously serve the Universal Light.

NOW I AM the Universal Light.
I AM the Universal Light.
I AM the Universal Light.
I AM—I AM—I AM.
I HAVE MERGED INTO THE ONENESS

MY SPIRITUAL CHAKRAS HAVE OPENED
And I know that
We are all one.
I am harmonized within the Universal Light.
Therefore, in the name of my Spiritual Being,
I choose to become one with all;

I AM a wave of vibrating Light
My Light Body is One with My Physical Body
Vibrating to the Frequency
Of the Fifth Dimension energies!

I AM

NOTES

CHAPTER SEVEN

Working With The Circle Of Light

SPONTANEOUS HEALING
Shedding Your Core Beliefs

The history of the Universe
Is a huge and ongoing process
Ever unfolding
As we grope and grow to the glory of Oneness.

We have discovered that false beliefs
Have limited us in the past
From enjoying optimum health,
reversing disease,
And creating loving, lasting relationships.

The Universe is a giant computer
And humans write the programming
With their thoughts and beliefs
Creating their reality.

Ascend as you uncover those thoughts
That bring peace, love, and harmony
To your life, your family,
Your community, and the World

—EAJ

A Spiritual revolution is occurring on this planet. Thousands of people are finding out from great teachers such as Louise Hay, Dr. Deepak Chopra, Gregg Braden, Caroline Myss, Dr. Eric Pearl, and one of my mentors, Stephen Lewis, (*Sanctuary*—the AIM Program), that what we think, just like what we eat, becomes and reflects who we are.

> *Our thoughts are things, moving energy fields, and we have been trained over and over again to think, act, and believe in certain ways. Letting go of these ingrained beliefs feels like falling off a speeding locomotive to certain death.*

Our Universe, the country, state, and town that we live in as well as our private home, is a creation of our inner belief system. This is what the current pre-Fifth Dimension revolution was about: the time before 2012. Now, suddenly we don't need someone else to tell us that we are a powerful part of this planet.

What many are currently looking for is not validation of the Ego. Instead, we are searching for the keys to unlock *the golden door of knowledge* within us and ascend to a higher vibration level. What is the key to applying our knowledge and creating a healthy daily life? We know we must learn this to survive, feel good about ourselves, and *Ascend* as well as claim our inner strength and power.

We are at a critical turning point that has been predicted since before man kept written records. And—surprise—we all *chose* to be born in this time and in this place. Great. Now what?

We need to see that self-healing, meditation practices, and positive thinking truly work. Then we need to accept this and our interactive role in the process. Rather than following the last few centuries teaching our limitations, we are opening up the first decade of the third millennium by embracing the fact that we are just the opposite. We are! We are the co-creators of our lives.

The Universe is made up of shared energy fields, which are all mixed within each dimension and they overlap one another. Within this higher energy field, people, animals, and things were once attached ethereally, and living as one energetic field of life.

Then everything became separated with *The Big Bang*, or simply the process of growth, we may never know, but there certainly was a division of energy and a newly created density within the electromagnetic fields. Many feel as if they should still be attached, which creates a longing inside to become whole again.

When we shift beliefs about our bodies, our lifestyle, our education, our accomplishments, and the World, the Divine energies support us in this change. With regard to healing, if the emotional cause of the illness is seen and accepted, the disease disappears. There is always a root cause, a moment of charge, an experience that creates every illness.

Because of an emotional imbalance, illness of the body is manifested from within us. Once the energy is balanced again and has changed within ourselves, the Chakra System brings a new reality into our lives. *Call it a mind-set upgrade; a disease free wellness.* Suddenly the impossible becomes possible just by setting a condition within our minds and believing it, unwaveringly.

William Vitalis, (Surya) taught me through the Clear Light Therapy course, that the root cause of illness may occur in a past life. JJ Dewey explains this in great detail in his book, *The Immortal.* In the Clear Light Therapy course, I was trained to give past life and present life regressions as a part of healing. These regressions had to be given in a certain way, by connecting my energy to the Divine through prayer, thought, and words.

Michelle came to me for a healing in 1987. She was in great fear because she had been diagnosed with multiple sclerosis. Michelle was only twenty-eight, married with a two-year-old son. I muscle-tested her and determined that she needed a present life therapy regression. We began the process.

I regressed Michelle back to age three, because that is usually a year of trauma, which creates an imprint on the shadow of the Soul. The trauma imprint remains in the aura until a trigger occurs in adult life, causing disease. I asked Michelle to remember her mother holding her.

Michelle began to sob and sob. She was able to explain that her mother was taken from her at that age, because she was ill. Her mother had a nervous breakdown because her brother had died of SIDS, sudden infant death syndrome. Instantly, I regressed Michelle back to age two, where she could remember the imprint of her mother holding her. This calmed her down.

Then a message came through me.

"Michelle, your son will not die of sudden infant death syndrome, and you will not have a nervous breakdown."

This came through me in a very powerful, piercing manner. I saw a bullet of Light hit Michelle in the Third Eye. She writhed for some time, and then her body became calm. At this point, I was certain that any disease regarding this trauma had been removed. Her face had changed. Every strain and worry mark had been removed, and she said she felt an inner peace. She looked beautiful.

A week later, Michelle called me to say that she felt terrific. Her energy had returned, and she no longer stumbled, wavered as she stood, or felt weak. Shortly after our session, she went back to the doctor for tests. The results showed that a healing had indeed taken place, although the doctor said that she had been misdiagnosed. To this day, Michelle is fine.

The human DNA contains all that we are. It is our blueprint in life, along with our astrological chart. The DNA record of the Body System, held within our bone marrow, is a double-edged sword; it holds the possibilities of our illness as well as the possibilities of our healing. As a baby, your DNA shows your past life history of preset illness possibilities, coming from your past lives and Soul ancestry.

These imprints may never become activated, and can be healed and removed from your Body System during the new lifetime. That is why they are there—to be experienced, healed, and removed for the growth of the Soul. However, we now know that these imbalances can be healed before they need to be experienced.

Through energy work or bodywork, your past life traumas, along with your ancestors', become healed. The Mormon Church teaches that all the ancestors of a member can be healed through their "special prayer" techniques. If this is true, then why can't the DNA imprints be cleared as well? They can be.

The human DNA directly influences what level you are vibrating at and what happens to you, experienced as your Karma, in a way that defies the perceived laws of time and space. Human beliefs can and do affect the

DNA within the Body System, which then influences the vibration and what occurs within the dimension you are living in as well as all the others.

In *John 14:2*, Jesus said, *"In my Father's house are many mansions: if it were not so, I would have told you. I go to prepare a place for you."* Each Soul ascends to its vibration level after death and dwells there, while processing for rebirth. The many mansions are the various Soul levels.

What is occurring in the Fifth Dimension, which is a Soul level, is the possibility of changing your natural DNA and removing the blocks that keep you from ascending and becoming who you really are—a loving, healing, and fully accomplished Child of the Universe. As you clear and cleanse, you Ascend to a higher place on Earth and go to a higher dimension at death. This is the basis of Clear Light Therapy and Radiant Healing.

These healing modalities are intense, spontaneous, and only flow from the Fifth Dimension. These energies, when used to heal, change your vibration, chakra spin and inner reality. They also remove the DNA imprint imbalances and the possibility of illness.

Stephen Lewis, co-author of *Sanctuary*, devised a way through electronics to work with your photograph and hold the DNA imprint in a state of perfection twenty-four hours a day, seven days a week. This is the AIM Program. With that advantage, the body can clear and heal naturally, along with your effort.

With this knowledge, the next question may be, "Are you really able to create and modify your body, lifestyle, or the world by your beliefs?" If so, the next question is, "What responsibility do you have to use this power at a time when you realize that you have created the greatest threats to your life, your future, your species, the planet, and perhaps this Solar System?"

Major scientists have concluded that we may not survive the twenty-first century without some kind of major setback to the human race. Stephen Lewis states, *"We have a new influence to contend with called 'human induced diseases or crises,' that must be taken into account as well."*

It is clear that we cannot continue on the way we have been going. We have entered a unique period in history where we can actually destroy not only our planet Earth, but also the Solar System where it resides.

The population is facing several major concerns: global health and energy consumption; disease and the human condition; food supply and delivery; technology and safety, along with the ever-expanding human race. We simply cannot expect to go on unless we begin to create some major changes.

Without a doubt, the future of humanity is created by millions of small, everyday decisions. It is usually on a daily basis where the most profound decisions are made, and there will be countless choices, which you all will be asked to make, in the not too distant future.

One of the simplest, yet most difficult challenges will be to embrace the new bandwidth, the energies of the Fifth Dimension; it is best to begin working with them now. Allow your past beliefs to graduate into new ones, and *realize who you are* and what your appropriate place is within the Universe. If you can accept that your thoughts and feelings, hidden deep within, are powerful evidence of what consciousness can do and the role it has in your future, then you can accept, change, and begin living a new life in a new world.

The missing link, what the Soul has forgotten, is that you are a part of the process and not separate from everything that you see and experience. That is why this Spiritual revolution and evolution is so powerful.

Since the tragedies of 9/11, we have been cast into a role of solving great crises of our time, rather than leaving them to future generations or casting them to the hands of fate. As we are the creators of our reality, we now know that we have the power to rearrange the atoms of matter itself.

What problems cannot be solved by working with this Fifth Dimension energy? What solutions could possibly be beyond our reach—those ideas, inspirations, talents, or desires that have not been thought of as yet, or those which have not entered into our consciousness or dimension?

How can we rewrite our current reality, and do we really have the power to do this? The ancient sages and mystics believed this truth: *we all have the power and possibility of healing and self-transformation*, and they taught these principles to their initiates. Why do we humans fear our own immortality or deny it? Can we not recognize that we are born with all of the powers to heal as well as share this knowledge with others?

One does not have to be specially anointed to be a healer or to pass on love and Spiritual awareness to others. Our thoughts, kindness, deeds, actions, and decisions will do just that. Only now, these miraculous changes will occur faster and faster, creating spontaneous healing.

In the nineteenth and twentieth centuries, we were taught that we are less than perfect. We are frail and powerless human beings who live in a world where things 'just happen' for no apparent reason. We were tempted: we sinned, did wrong, and believed we could go unpunished. Then suddenly our Karma caught up with us. After the 1960's there has been more of a focus on self-responsibility.

Our Gurus and Sages teach that there is a force hiding deep within us that has a power that no one can touch. Our Spirit, or Soul, cannot be broken. However, we don't take the time to access this power. Just as the surgeon has to cut and stitch, so we must have courage to take the time to slow down, stop, and delve within for our healing.

Jesus said, *"Watch and pray, that ye enter not into temptation: the Spirit indeed is willing, but the flesh is weak."* (*Matt. 26: 41*)

Sometimes we are victims of circumstance, and other times we are a powerful force. The secret lies in the power of our decisions. *"What are we going to believe in, success or failure?"* Dick Summer

We have been given the Divine ability to create our own reality. Everything we experience in our daily life, past lives, and future lives is based on the power of our decisions, NOW. We can change our core beliefs. In her book *You Can Heal Your Life*, Louise Hay points out that our thoughts and deep beliefs about ourselves can change our circumstances, our relationships, as well as our disease.

Healing false beliefs that have limited you in the past, or shedding, as Dr. Eric Pearl calls it in *The Reconnection,* will uncover thoughts that bring peace into your life, family, community, and the world. It isn't easy and we all resist this process hanging on to old, outdated beliefs as if we would die without them. You think it has to be true because he or she said so. No truer words were spoken than this song from *South Pacific*:

You've got to be taught
To hate and fear
You've go to be taught
Year by year
It's got to be drummed in your dear little ear,
You've got to be carefully taught.

You've got to be taught
To be afraid
Of people whose eyes are oddly made
Or people whose skin is a different shade
You've got to be carefully taught!
—Rogers and Hammerstein

We have already seen that hate, fear, war, and disease can destroy life faster than anything. But, do we have the courage to look within and accept our power to overcome this? Will we change our beliefs, our way of living, our consciousness, even if we must pass through a "living death" to do so?

Traditional medicine, surgery, and confinement may be some steps to heal, but NONE of these services reach and penetrate the Soul.

Louise Hay believes and teaches that by transforming our destructive beliefs of the past and replacing them with life-affirming ones of healing and peace, we can transform our lives, the world, and the future consciousness of *all that is*.

While working with her on the Healing Hay Rides of the 1980's, it became apparent to thousands that *what we think can begin to uplift us and change the outcome of our lives.* Overcoming fear and not allowing it to consume us is key, as that is what holds us back.

With the help of bodywork, affirmations, singing, dancing, and honest sharing, lives shifted, disease left the body, and some people walked away free, healthy, happy, and clear.

Dr. Deepak Chopra, another one of my teachers, took it all a daring step further in the 1990's. He explained that we can visualize an outcome, bring that thought into our body system, and it will manifest. Amazing. Can it be done? Yes, but it takes time, and most of us give up beforehand, because it's not instant.

People simply do not realize what it takes to expose a jewel. We have to dig and dig, move resistant rocks and dirt, and then find the "diamond in the rough" and process it before it can shine for us. Receiving your Spiritual blessings is not like getting fast food at MacDonald's. To make significant belief changes takes dedication, faith, time, and the true belief that we are Children of the Universe and deserve only the best.

There are human energy fields and cycles within the levels of each dimension. Each one of these fields is a course of study within itself. These fields may be considered a place where Soul change can occur. There is an entire science, a very exact science, based upon the access and use of these Light patterns, individually and as composite fields. Each time an individual form is accessed and its vibration is lifted and purified, all fields of that form (timelines, ancestors, and original family) are also accessed and lifted through a resonance, deep within the Soul.

Higher selves communicate with other higher selves naturally, which is why you like some people when you meet them and feel fear or repulsion toward others. You may meet someone and like him instantly, or feel as if you have met him before. This is called *Soul recognition,* because you have spent many lifetimes together.

The Blessed Higher Self has the power to heal and enlighten you. Many of you have a burning desire to become enlightened now because you want to offer good service, gain wisdom and knowledge as well as expand and grow. Because of the new energies arriving on this planet over the next several years, the life experience now includes gaining access to the power and vibration of the Fifth Dimension, the dimension of spontaneous healing.

There is a new vibrational healing, energetic flow arriving from the Fifth Dimension that will make most other healing modalities passé. A new science is emerging that recognizes that living things operate in sync to a rhythm of life. This is why some of us like classical music while others prefer rock or rap.

The musical notes, when put together, can give you an electrical pull, or harmonious feeling at whatever vibration you are vibrating to. Richard Shulman, composer and musician, believes that *"...listening to higher dimensional music can help to raise the consciousness into a place of healing and wholeness to spontaneously heal."*

Certainly that is what occurs when William Vitalis sings from the Soul. The room's energy is changed and you can actually feel the vibrations of love. The power and strength of the music is sometimes too much for people. They cannot take in the music because it hurts the body by causing pain and discomfort. They simply are not vibrating at the level this music creates.

The influence of time and certain periodic cycles affect the Body System. The human pulse, blood pressure, body temperature, circulation of the lymphocytes, and hormonal cycles appear to ebb and flow according to some sort of recurring timetable. These rhythms are not unique to humans, but dwell in animals as well as all nature.

The difference between humans and nature is that nature does this instinctively, while we humans fight to get back into balance. We constantly run on adrenal energy, putting off getting still to readjust our inner rhythms and calming ourselves down to a place of quiet within.

We refuse to get the proper rest and exercise, eat nutritional foods, and listen to the messages from our bodies. Are we not missing something, perhaps, harmony with all things, by not following our biological rhythms or internal clock? What a fabulous mechanism our bodies are.

The mental body is concerned with *knowledge* or *concrete thinking*, while the ethereal body is concerned with *wisdom*, which comes from its many lifetime experiences. The Higher Self brings us *insights,* which are clear and help us alter and purify our perceptions of truth.

If we would listen to all three of them together, we might come together. If we knew more about this science of recognizing living things and operate in Oneness to a rhythm of life, would we self-heal? Is there a way we can know this instinctively like nature does?

Now that we are living in a new century, the process has changed to another higher octave. Reconnecting with the Soul or becoming one with your Blessed Higher Self removes all fear, blocks, and any other interference. Yes, the Fifth Dimension energies are manifesting.

Stand back. It may take awhile, but the healings you are doing, the lives you touch, enhance, balance, and help to heal are about to become mainstream and in high demand. Expect people to come to you from far away places; clients will call, and you will be very busy with your energy healing work. Why?—because this healing process works like nothing else.

Circle of Light Meditation

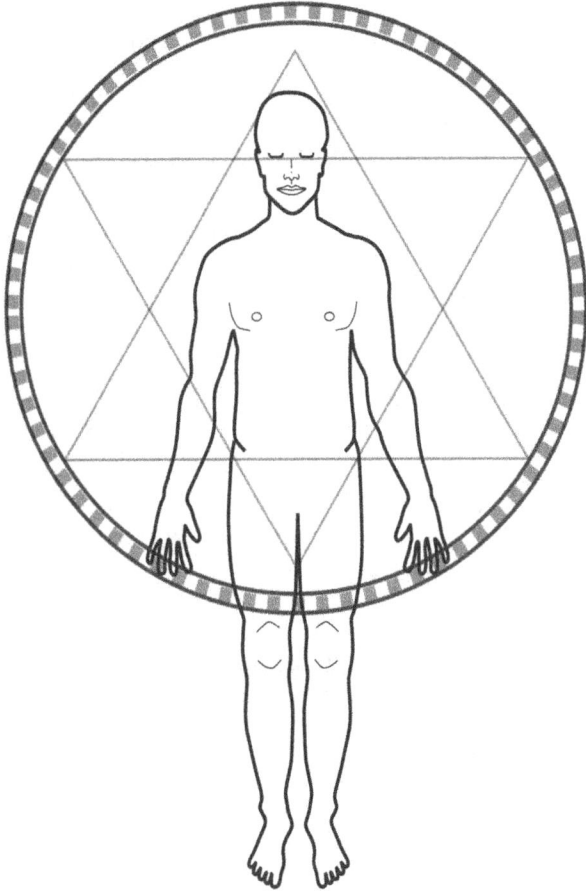

(EH)

Circle of Light Meditation

This meditation technique is more powerful and successful than any other I know of. Sit, get quiet, and precede this meditation by doing the complete pre-requisite preparation exercises in the back of this book, beginning with the Sat Nam and ending by wrapping with the White Light, then begin the Circle of Light Meditation. You will be in a clear space and a higher vibration.

To use the *Circle of Light Meditation*, sit in a chair, feet flat on the floor, keeping your spine straight, your legs uncrossed. Close your eyes and begin to picture a "Circle of Light" in front of you, through your Third Eye. Allow the energies of the new crystal Fifth Dimension Third Eye to be placed in the center of your third eye.

What is the problem you need solved or the relationship you need healed? Think of the problem, disturbance, or upset holding a picture of it in your mind. Then wait—be aware of the colors you see present—and then begin to see the problem being solved to bring relief, peace, and harmony to the situation. Ask that the problem—can be anything, from a broken marriage, lost love, fear of your job, lack of money, a need for physical healing, or whatever is upsetting you at the moment – be resolved in Divine Order. Hold the outcome – wait for the Light in the circle to become bright; a bright, golden yellow.

Then come out of the meditation and simply go on about your business, allowing the Universe to work out the energetic process for you, and a completely new frequency. Trust the Universe. This process may take you twenty to thirty minutes, but the results are amazing.

Distant Healing

Need first name, birth date, and geographical location of client. Sit at a table and position the *Golden Light Manifestation* rod at the lower back of the neck. *Create a Circle of Light* on the table in front of you. Place your client(s) face up inside the circle with their head to your left, feet to your right.

It is best to clear yourself before doing any healing modality on others. Begin with bringing in White Light through the Crown chakra. Then work your Chakras, one at a time, including the Eighth Chakra, and possibly the Ninth if you feel that one is open and spinning for you. (Do the pre-requisite meditation in the back of this book if possible.)

Add the mantra, *I open to the service of the Divine*. Complete your session with the breath of fire, and then surround yourself with White Light, to clear away any negative energy residue. This clearing exercise should be done every day if you are in the healing services.

When healing more than one person at a time, place clients (up to 12 at one session) atop each other in an offset manner, with 1" space between the energetic bodies.

After completion, do the breath of fire again and wrap yourself with White Light. This will clear and release any energy that may have clung to you or is still lingering in the atmosphere.

See diagram following.

Distant Ascension Vibrational Healing

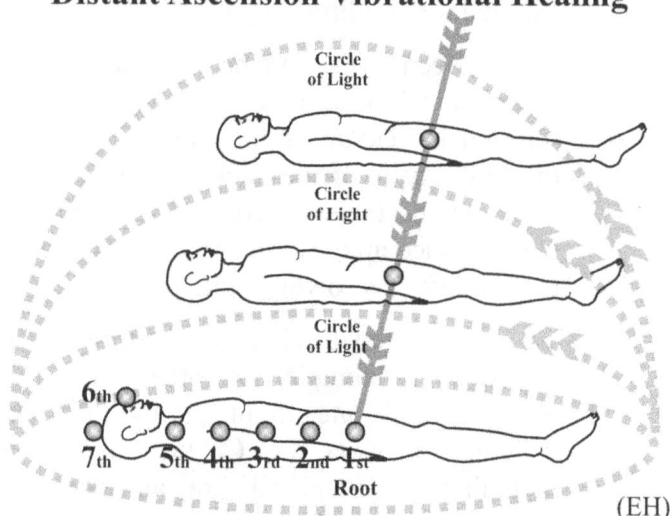

Circle
of Light

Circle
of Light

Circle
of Light

6th

7th 5th 4th 3rd 2nd 1st

Root

(EH)

You can send Divine Seals via Distant Healing by using either the Third Eye (for one person) or photographs. You can send to as many as twelve people at one time. Begin with the Root Chakra, setting the photos on a diagonal line. Moving upwards, apply each Seal to its respective Chakra. The *Golden Amber Light Ray* will penetrate each Chakra point simultaneously.

After you apply the Divine Seals, return to the foot of the photograph, then visualize the *Violet Ray*. Begin a clockwise *Circle of Light* at the feet, with the Violet Ray. Move up the Body along the midline to about 6 inches above the Crown Chakra, staying within the aura field. Then do another circle near the top of the aura field, in the fourth level of the aura, in the amber light, if you can sense that. This is the *Fifth Dimension Violet Ray of Light* will hold the Seals in place and add extra balancing energy.

Complete each client by wrapping the *Golden/Amber Light Arch* over their entire body. This both strengthens the aura, and holds the energy in place, so that the effects can permeate through the body system at will; creating balance, health, and a refreshing energy, over a period of time.

This *Ascension Vibrational Energy Healing* process is able to drain off or to detoxify and cleanse the human cells, organs, and systems of the many toxins and invaders, which are causing these imbalances.

The mean for beginners is five to seven days before a "recharge" may be necessary.

The following is an example of a Fifth Dimension healing:

From the time I was a small child I knew that I could heal, see the future, alter my reality through prayer and meditation, and that I had past lives. I could see waves of energy in the atmosphere and instinctively knew if the air was polluted. I could concentrate and increase my ability to visualize as well as have the power to cure my illness or someone else's. None of this felt strange or uncomfortable to me. I thought everyone could do these things.

If I was concerned about the health of someone I loved, I would lay his ethereal body down in the center of the palm of my right hand, head touching the top of my middle finger, feet touching my wrist.

Then I would cover this body with my left hand and send it Light through the center of my Third Eye. I would hold this energy until I felt the ethereal body was saturated with Light, and instinctively I would know if a healing had begun. I did this lovingly and often throughout my life, never knowing that I was already working with the Fifth Dimension energies.

In 1991 I had a falling out with a false teacher. I lost my 'self.' I felt unworthy and was in 'Spiritual shock' for more than three months. I could not go out of my condo and was praying and meditating constantly. Finally, my minister sent me up to his cabin on Cape Cod to heal. I was there for ten days, playing the bhajan *Ardas* (prayer beyond prayer), until my body gave me a signal that it was over. I had been able to repurify myself.

I returned to my condo in Mahwah, New Jersey, wondering what was ahead for me. That night I said a prayer and asked for guidance. I asked God to show me the way. Was I to continue my Spiritual teaching and healing work, or was this false teacher right? Was I "spit out of the sky?" Had I somehow become unworthy? I fervently asked God for an answer, telling Him I would accept and abide by whatever He wanted for me.

The next day was Sunday, and around ten-o'clock in the morning the phone rang. It was a new client who wanted to come by with her sister for a reading. I gladly accepted the appointment. That afternoon Pat and Karen came in and sat down in the living room. Pat was from Ramsey, the next town over. I noticed she talked funny and asked her what had happened.

She had lockjaw from a car accident six years ago. Evidently the clavicle had taken the shock of the impact and had moved out of place, or rather out of alignment with the chakras. She had not eaten solid food since.

I gave the readings, and as the girls were leaving, I reached out and touched Pat's arm.

"Sometimes when I touch people, something happens. May I touch your face?"

She looked into my eyes and sensed my sincerity. As I reached up and touched both cheeks with the open palm of my hands, a bullet of Light shot through my body, entered the Crown Chakra and traveled down through the soles of my feet. We both went into a trance, swaying back and forth to the rhythm of the energy waves.

Closing my eyes, I saw three little angels in white on each side of Pat's face, cleaning out negative energy from her jaw. We swayed for about ten minutes. The angels cleaned out both sides of the jaw, and then I visualized hosing out the inside space with water, filled it with Light, and plated it with silver plates to hold in the Light. Then it was done.

When I dropped my hands, Pat's jaw opened and closed several times. She was healed. With tears in her eyes, she went into my altar room for a few minutes. I suggested that she look into the mirror and thank herself for having the courage to 'drop' her illness.

She returned in a few minutes, and we both were suddenly filled with joy and laughter. After Pat returned home, she called to thank me again, saying that she was eating an apple for the first time in six years. My heart sang because I realized that last night's prayer had been answered.

Be sure to celebrate and show gratitude to Spirit. When you celebrate, you acknowledge to Spirit that you have chosen to be a channel for this new bandwidth of energy and are thankful. It is a good idea for you to allow those healed to thank you in their own way and for you to accept their gift of thanks graciously.

You must do this for their sake. By doing so, you help create joy and thankfulness.

Pat was enthralled with her healing experience, as are many. She came to the meditation group a few times afterward. However, she did not continue, nor did she return to her church. You see, some people 'get something' out of having a disease. Hanging on to a disease is subconscious and sometimes brings more attention from loved ones, along with special compensation, disability benefits, or whatever.

If Pat were *cured* she would have to be more responsible. She would have to return to her life prior to having lockjaw. Having that negative special attention was something she did not want to give up.

We now know that our inner beliefs affect everything within our DNA, body systems, and our immune system. Our belief system affects our world, whoever comes into our lives, and the life we build around us.

We are born with the power to reverse disease, while creating peace and abundance. We can change our own vision of reality! Even Buddha taught that *every human being is the author of his own health or disease.*

Of course, the key is in the reprogramming we need to accomplish within ourselves. It begins with a single thought. Pat did not want to invest in herself, for whatever reason. On some level, Pat thought she needed her lockjaw and the Universe supported that thought.

Today, Pat is fine, but the lockjaw returned after about a year or so. It's not as severe as it had been, but nonetheless, the lesson here is not physical but, indeed, a Spiritual one.

Gregg Braden states in *The Spontaneous Healing of Belief,* "We are not on the sidelines of our life, but the actual players. We are in the same program we are trying to change."

What we say and what we think create our reality within ourselves as well as within the world in which we live; always remember that the Universe always supports us.

NOTES

CHAPTER EIGHT

Accessing Your Akashic Records

WIKIPEDIA*: Akashic records (from akasha, the Sanskrit word for 'sky' 'space' or 'ether') are a compendium of mystical knowledge supposedly encoded in a non-physical plane known as the astral plane.*

The term Akashic Records entered the language of theosophy through H. P. Blavatsky, who characterized it as a sort of life force; she also referred to "indestructible tablets of the astral light" recording both the past and future of human thought and action, but she did not explicitly identify these as "akashic" in nature.

The notion of an akashic *record* is attributed to Alfred Percy Sinnett, who, in his book *Esoteric Buddhism*, wrote of a Buddhist belief in "a permanency of records in the Akasa" and "the potential capacity of man to read the same."

By C. W. Leadbeater's *Clairvoyance* the association of the term with the idea was complete, and he identified the akashic records by name as something a clairvoyant, or a highly trained energetic healer, could read.

From the "Akasha," a Sanskrit word and meaning "primary substance" — that out of which all things are formed. These Records are known in every Spiritual tradition. For example, in the Judeo-Christian tradition as both *"The Book of Life"* and *"The Book of God's Remembrance."*

#

Souls are eternal. This life is not the first life you have lived on this earth and most likely will not be your last. Your past lives have taught you about life, about yourself, and have helped you reach the level of perfection and Soul alignment you have attained up to this point. Your body is finite and you have come here with goals you wish to achieve in this lifetime.

Because there is so much more to you than one body can hold for the brief time that you have on Earth, you have only brought with your consciousness a small amount of knowledge, skills, aptitude and wisdom from the everything that you have become in your past lives; just enough to help you be successful, and as much as you could hold during the process of birth and childhood. However, in these new energies, you are able to remember and experience more of who you truly are.

Our past lives work with and inform our present life in many ways, including influencing our opinions, our perspectives, and what we *know to be true* even though we have never experienced it in this life. These stored records are the basics from which we build our personalities in this life.

Through a Past Life Regression you can remember and reintegrate who and where your Soul has been and the wisdom you have gained through your past life experiences. You can release old hurts that you have held in your Soul through traumatic events that have again manifested in your current body. You can recognize Soulmates and acquaintances and make sense of seemingly random likes and dislikes, music, or collections that you have been attracted to and have established for years.

WHAT ARE THE AKASHIC RECORDS?

The Akashic records are like the DNA of the Universe. They are the Soul's journey over time, so every thought, word, and deed is registered in the Akashic records. Each Soul has its own Akashic record, and there are collective records of all Souls on all journeys.

The way we receive information from the Akashic Records is in encoded Light language, which is the sacred geometry of words encoded in a certain frequency; learning how to interpret this information is crucial. We can start learning to use our inner senses to give words and interpretation to what we receive; we can also start getting fine-tuned to this new energy through meditation and past life regression work. The information in the Akashic Records helps us bring our past, present and future into the "now," and thus into our consciousness. By accessing the Akashic records, we can identify and release anything negative that we have created; any past action or energetic mass that has become a block to our present realization of our oneness with God.

We can look at why we have addictive patterns, why we choose the relationships we do, why we have created our habitual responses, over and over again. We can learn how to create new, positive actions in our lives, by making new decisions instead of the old knee-jerking re-action.

The Akashic Records refer to a database of every word, thought or action that is stored energetically and encoded in a non-physical plane of existence. They are said to contain the information of every Soul in the cosmos. The Records are continually updated, with each new thought, word or action that every Soul or entity makes. The Akashic Records therefore contain the energetic blueprints about the origination and journey of every Soul through its lifetimes. They connect each of us to one another.

Akasha is a Sanskrit word meaning "sky", "space" or "ether". To aid in visualization, most describe the Akashic

Records metaphorically as a library. Others likened it to be a *Universal Computer, the Mind of God,* the *Cosmic or Collective Consciousness*, the *Collective Unconscious* or the *Collective Subconscious*. Akashic Records are not physically an out-there thing. It is the speck of Divinity within us that allows us to access the field of the Akashic Records.

Everything about the Universe has an energetic record. The records of your Soul are located via your full name at birth, hour of birth, and birth date of this current lifetime. That is the key that unlocks the door, plus your Soul vibration. The records are embedded with information about your previous lifetimes, your Soul origination, pre-set current life lessons and your Soul purpose, and also about future choice points.

The Soul's journey of self-awareness is undertaken through a cause and effect process. You are constantly presented with opportunities to meet Self and to apply Spiritual principles in the physical world. You will meet with lessons that will be provided again and again, until you have gained Soul-mastery.

These records can be accessed through being in a deep state of consciousness or meditation. Anyone can have access to their personal Akashic Record. It is like having an internet access to the same database of information.

In reality, no special powers or abilities are needed to get into the Akashic Records. The same records are accessible by the subconscious mind through dreams, intuitive insight, and energetic exercises. However, a cluttered mind, ego, little connection with one's Higher Self, and a lack of trust in one's Divine power, are hindrances that an Akashic Record reader needs to overcome first. It is only when there is complete harmony between the conscious, subconscious, or super-conscious mind that Truth from the Akashic Records can be accessed and understood. If you are a beginner is it always safe and best to work with a healing professional.

One of the best is Luisa Rasiej. She is located in Bucks County, PA. Her website is www.theinnercontessa.com.

One of the most famous of Akashic Record readers is the late American psychic Edgar Cayce (1877-1945). He has been called the "sleeping prophet," the "father of holistic medicine," and is about the most documented psychic of the Twentieth Century. He has done readings on more than 10,000 topics, including some incredible healing techniques.

Other famous personalities who have accessed the Akashic Records include Nostradamus, Quatzlcoatl, Rudolph Steiner, Mary Baker Eddy, and Emmanuel Swedenbord.

Readings from the Akashic Records
You can read the Akashic Records from the your present Time Line. All about the past, present and future is brought into the "Now" to be read. You get a glimpse into the journey and the path of your Soul through the Universe. When you read into your Akashic Records you

understand that your Soul has a voice. This can help to identify what past traumas and obstructions that have left a negative energetic imprint. By doing so, you can call on the power of Divine Grace and set an intention to release them.

Soul access to these records is indeed a powerful way to raise your energy vibrations. It is an important key to becoming Spiritually Whole. Your *being* walks in greater awareness from the time you clear your Akashic Records. It is less important to know who you have once been. It is who you are and who you are in the process of becoming that is of greater significance. The Soul's past and a sense of who you are at Soul level now, provide a framework of information with which to work at alignment and raising your vibration. What you ultimately do with the knowledge is always a matter of free will and choice.

In each lifetime, you undergo experiences which can enable your Soul to connect back to the Divine. The ultimate benefit of finding out what is held in your own Akashic Records is essentially to realize your Oneness with God, The Universe, and Divine Spirit.

Working with the Akashic Records is one of the most powerful tools available on the planet today, to help us remember our oneness with our Divine Source.

- How to access the Akashic Records is rarely taught.

- Below is a description of a highly valuable process you can use to open the

Akashic Records, with training, or through an energetic healer.

- You can read Akashic Records for the Self and, with training and Divine permission, you can use this awareness to guide another to open the records for themselves.

- This process is so rich with information that some people just use this access as a primary way to read for clients. This is known as a *straight psychic* reading as is rarely wrong.

- Along with using the Akashic Records for readings and guidance about Soul direction, you can also manifest with Akashic Records information.

- Among the Leadbeater's book *Man: How, Whence, and Whither?* He claims to have recorded the history of Atlantis and other civilizations as well as the future society of Earth in the 28th century.

- Rudolf Steiner, Austrian, philosopher, social reformer, architect, and esotericist, referred to the Akashic records and reported about Atlantis, Lemuria, and the evolution of man and Earth, et cetera.

- Levi H. Dowling's *Aquarian Gospel of Jesus the Christ* offers a version of the youth of Jesus Christ ostensibly based upon Akashic record material.

- In *The Law of One, Book I*, a book purported to contain conversations with a channeled "social memory complex" known to humans as Ra, when the questioner asks where Edgar Cayce received his information, the answer received is,

  "We have explained before that the intelligent infinity is brought into intelligent energy from the sixth density or octave. The one soul vibratory complex called Edgar used this gateway to view the present, which is not the continuum you experience but the potential social memory complex of this planetary sphere. The term your people have used for this is the "Akashic Record" or the "Hall of Records."

  (According to Cayce, access to this *Hall of Records* is located between the paws of the Sphinx, in Giza, in Egypt.)

Past-life regression work and tapping into the Akashic Records brings us comprehensive insight into the root causes behind the persistent negative patterns of thought, emotion, and behavior that plague so many people. By examining negative blocks and restrictions that may be affecting us at Soul-level, we can gain real and meaningful explanations for many of our present-life experiences.

Best of all, through this powerful method of Spiritual healing, we can clear and heal negative blocks that are limiting people at Soul-level. Through working with your personal energy field and the Divine Seals, people experience a profound transformation in their life experiences. They begin attracting new experiences. They create more of what they want. They break through to a new level of Spiritual growth and evolution. (See: *Ascension—Accessing The Fifth Dimension-WORKBOOK*)

ADJUSTING YOUR SOUL CONSCIOUSNESS

Adjusting and realigning your Soul consciousness is very specific. It involves tapping into your Akashic Records through the modality of energetic healing and past-life regression. Through energy work and muscle testing, the healer is able to access very specific information within your cellular memory, which is key to accessing your personal Akashic Records.

The first step is to find out who your Soul is at an energetic level, how it was created, and what vibration level the Soul is in at this time. Your records will inform you as to when you first became an expression of the Divine. This knowledge tells you about your Soul level gifts as well as your Divine nature so that you can start living your Divine purpose.

The other piece of information is about what choices have been made both in this lifetime as well as in your past lives. These choices have set up definite patterns within you.

All of us have set up some negativity in our lives, which is somehow blocking us from really living our Soul's Divinity. The good news is that once we discover this negativity and how it was created, we can clear away these blocks both for ourselves as well as others.

You may be asking, "How can our Akashic Records tell us who we really are at Soul level?" Well, what is read in the Soul at this level is your origination; that moment when you were first created from the Divine or God source. This was the birth of your Soul, the moment you became an individual expression of the Divine. The Akashic Records contain all the information about your Soul, from the inception way up to this present lifetime. This expression is your original Divine nature.

Souls go to every area of our Galaxy when they originate, and through many of the vibrationary levels. (See *Ascension—Accessing The Fifth Dimension*). They need to experience themselves in many kinds of expressions. When a Soul comes to the Earth plane, it has chosen to experience itself through physical form. This is a definite choice all of us made on the planet.

There are many, many Souls on Earth who did not begin their Soul journey here. In fact, if you're reading this book right now, most likely your Soul did not originate on the Earth plane. This modality of learning and accessing the higher levels, usually attract Soul travelers almost exclusively. Broaden your scope and realize that the Soul can express itself at or within other places besides Earth.

Basically, when you look at your Akashic Records during a Soul adjustment you can "see" or be informed of where the Soul originated. Where did your Soul have its very first expression? This is important information because each Star System has its own energetic quality. The Star System of your origination brings forth valuable information about your individuality and particular qualities. This is based on the Natural Law of *Like attracts like*. The Soul makes a decision, and all life begins with a decision. The Soul chooses a location, a Star System, that is most like itself, and one that it is vibrationaly aligned to. Souls who share the same origination actually have a lot in common. They are vibrationaly in tune and harmonize with each other. So knowing our Soul's origination, where they came from, brings insight as to who and what they are at Soul level.

When a Soul first becomes a Soul, when Divine Source creates the Soul as an individual expression of itself, then it *becomes*, and has a specific expression as well as specific gifts and attributes. The Soul is then a perfect expression of the Divine, absolutely perfect.

Therefore, the concept of Soul evolution, development, or the growth of our Soul is in error. Our Souls don't really need to develop at all. All Souls are perfect, unique expressions of the Divine. A Soul doesn't have to become a more evolved Soul, nor does it need to learn lessons. Now, many of us are very attached to the concept of "going to school" on this earth plane. Do not become upset about this new information. Although our Souls don't have to evolve or learn, the human race and physical body expression of the Soul does! The human part of us needs to grow, learn, and gain wisdom. Our Souls, on the other hand, are Divine, beautiful, unique, and a perfect expression of themselves.

Let's take a closer look. The Soul originates and is perfect. Now you may ask, "Okay, then why bother to create a new Soul? If you are Divine Source and you are everything and everywhere, then there is nothing that you are not. So how would you experience yourself if you're everything? You do this by creating things that are of you, but not you. Divine Source creates a Soul to become an individual aspect of itself, but not all. It is only through your Divine Contract that the Divine Source can experience itself.

In order to experience our Selves we also must experience what we are not, the difference between us and the rest of creation. That's why the Divine creates Souls, to experience itself in different aspects and forms.

The Soul is made up of energetic frequencies that flow through it. Some of us have a stronger frequency in one area and are weaker in another, and another Soul would have that weaker frequency strongly aspected, which is what makes each one of us, even identical twins, unique. None of us are exactly alike. We each have our own Spiritual Blueprint, contained in the 9th Chakra, which holds our Spiritual DNA, or a part of our Akashic Record.

The Soul makes the decision to be created in order to experience itself. *We all have the same Soul purpose, to experience ourselves.* We then witness our own nature and create our experiences through choice. That's what living is every day. Making choices that align with our Divine nature. This is why knowing yourself at Soul level is very important. This is a must if you want to walk your Divine path.

To learn about the Akashic Records is a choice of diving in deeply to learn and know about our Soul's Divine nature. When we are born into a new life, most of us have totally forgotten who we are. We feel as if we are in separation with the Divine. We are not living and doing that which we really are. We've forgotten all that was. That is why we create less than Divine experiences for ourselves.

We struggle with money, health, or relationships. There is nothing Divine about worrying how to pay our bills or being in pain in our bodies. However, since December 21st, 2012, we are living in an exciting time. With the arrival of the new double-helix energies from the Fifth Dimension, we have a chance to, collectively, become aware that we are Spiritual beings.

Now, some of us are being called to go beyond the general realization that we are Spirit. We are called to go deeper and to begin to understand what it really means to be a Spiritual being. We are being asked to step into a new level of Spiritual identification and get to know our Soul at its true level. Then we can reach out and help everyone else do the same. That is why many of us choose to become Spiritual healers.

This is what Spiritual evolution is all about. It's about aligning our human experience, evolving our egos so that we can make conscious choices that align with the perfection of our Soul. Understanding our karma and astrological chart becomes important here, as it helps us verify and accept the responsibility for the challenges offered on this current life path on Earth. We align and begin living in practical ways, raise our vibration and harmonics to become One with our Soul. To do that, we need to know what our Soul even is, and how we can apply that understanding.

Spiritual growth is not about becoming more. No, it's about coming back to who we really are and have always been. Your Soul profile is a combination of your past-life karma and the pattern challenges in your astrological birth chart. In that combination, the Souls becomes a perfect expression of the Divine. When you read about yourself, then you will get a clear picture of what your Soul is in its Divine perfection. As we get to know who our Soul really is, we will learn who the Souls around us are. When we can see others around us as who they really are, and ourselves as who we really are, miracles happen.

We understand how we are alike, and how we are different. Our relationships improve because we can know and understand where others are coming from. Perhaps we realize that our child must have structure, yet be allowed to play because that's a part of their Divine being.

Imagine living with your parents, spouse, lover, or boss who can see you in your Divinity. Their knowledge comes through how they treat you, communicate with you, and allow you to be in your brilliance, and also by knowing what your brilliance is not. Knowing what you're not gifted in can be just as valuable as understanding what your gifts are.

That's the difference between all of us. Understanding who other Souls are, where they came from, and their Divine expressions, helps us accept and not be judgmental. Many of us feel good with this information and accept it easily. There is a marker in our Akashic Records, like a road sign, that tells us who we are at Soul level. This information tells us about our specific Divine gifts, our brilliance, and our Soul purpose. This information is unbelievably accurate.

Also, we come in Soul groups, which is good information and can help our relationships. For example, your family members may not be in the Soul group you came from. This knowledge can help you honor them, and be accepting of their differences. Then you can support them in their life style. By witnessing, by tuning into the vibrational differences between ourselves and the people around us, we get to know ourselves even better. Not only with them, but we can also give ourselves permission to be just who we truly are. *Then we can give everyone around us permission to be who they truly are,* and that is an amazing gift to provide for our loved ones. That's what stepping into our power and our gifts is all about. We allow ourselves to show up as Divine beings within this human experience. Life is no longer "trying to fit in," or "trying to make sense of ourselves," because it all gets revealed.

Your Soul also has energy centers, which tell you about where your vibrational spectrum is. The frequencies your Soul is made of tell you how you were designed by the Divine to manifest and live this human experience, what your gifts are, and what your Soul's purpose is all about. This is all contained within your Akashic Soul profile.

Most of us are not living our Soul's purpose or profile because we have forgotten who we really are. Did you ever wonder why there is so much negativity around? Let's examine just why that happens, in detail.

EXPRESSING NEGATIVITY

Notice your resistance to that word Negativity–do not run from it–understand it. No one can deny that there is a lot of negativity on our planet. When you turn on the news it usually brings in fear, fear, fear.

Now–be assured that there are no negative forces conspiring against you. There is no actual barrier between Light and dark. There really is no struggle because there is no enemy. We are not here to struggle against negativity because it is not working against us.

Yes, negativity exists, but it's nothing to struggle against. So, you may ask, "Why is there negativity in our lives?" Negativity is in our lives because of the choices that we have made, in one lifetime or another. We chose it. That thought may make you uncomfortable at first. You think, "No way did I choose this for myself." Especially when it comes to our financial negativity.

The up side is that because we've chosen negativity, we can change it. We have the power to do so. We can change our choices at any time and at any given moment. We chose our negativity, and we can unclaim it and turn our lives around. But first, we need to understand what negativity is, accept it, understand how we create it, and then begin to make different choices and take different steps.

If we didn't create negativity, then we have no power over it. Instead of realizing this Truth, we begin to battle against it, and that's like starting a fight with ourselves. Or we invent some crazy stories about how the negative forces are working against us. Believe me, I am asked about this all the time.

If negativity is outside of us, a force to battle against, then we have already disempowered ourselves. Let me explain how this occurs. Negativity is nothing, in fact it's less than nothing. Negativity is the absence of Light.

Remember that you are a Divine Being, and at some point you have made a choice to act against nature and your natural flow. You have made a choice to be and act a certain way. Perhaps you have accepted the thought "I am nothing and deserve to live without." That's a negative choice.

Let's just say that at the Soul level you are a healer. You work with Divine Light and healing. Then as you grow, other influences and thoughts come along. Perhaps as a teenager you were told, "Well, that's not really practical. You have to grow up and get a real job," and you feel forced to buy into that limited belief system that you culture believes in.

Now you are grown up, have that job and life style, and spend fifty to sixty hours a week being who your Soul is not. You made a choice against your own special and Divine expression, and you are being who you are not! Not only that, you hate your job, your defense is, "Well, no one else really likes their job either, so, ahhhh." Then you shrug your shoulders. "That's okay," you murmur with your head down.

Well –IT'S NOT! It is truly not okay, because you are choosing everyday to act against yourself. You are choosing to be who you are not. The fact is you could leave your job. You could shift your life into its authentic expression as a healer, which is who you are at the Soul level. Then your Divinity would be expressed by doing some version of healing work.

However, every day you choose to go back to that job. You choose to take an action based on who you are not, based on the outer world's belief system. We are very powerful as human beings and we can act against our own nature. That is Natural Law because of free will, and the *Law of Polarity*, which we came here to experience. All Souls on planet Earth can choose to experience themselves as Divine or as not Divine. We can live in our positive or negative self-expression. It's a free choice!

Negativity is not something in and of itself. It's not evil and it's not an invisible force. Actually it's the absence of Self. This planet needs negativity. One of the laws that govern this Solar System, and perhaps this Universe, is the *Law of Polarity*. Polarity is how we compare, contrast, and experience. How can we experience who we are if there is no example of who we are not?

Positive and Negative are just two sides of the same coin. There is nothing bad about it. Duality exists so that we can choose the positive. If we didn't have the negative, then we would not be aware that there is a positive that we can choose. Natural Law states that *negativity arises when we make choices that align with what and who we are not.*

We choose to stay in relationships that don't express our Divine nature, or work in jobs that we are not happy with; or in religions and educational institutions, and we've been doing this for lifetime after lifetime., unfortunately.

Here is an example of giving in to fear after you have aligned with your Soul, set a condition, and then gone against yourself.

One of my close friends, Iris, was selling her home in the Germantown area of Philadelphia. She was discouraged because she was receiving little or no offers, and because the offers made were way under her desired price. She called me and asked what to do, and if I thought I could be of any help.

Iris was certainly feeling stuck. I knew she needed a clearing of the negative forces first. Iris meditates and is very Spiritually savvy. We both did a clearing together on the telephone. Then, as we felt the clear energy coming in, I instructed her to "set a condition." Tell her Blessed Higher Self what she needed to sell the house for, the exact amount, and then close her eyes and visualize the sale. See the closing papers being signed and the check, in that amount, being handed to her. We did that together as well. The union of our energies strengthened the condition.

I reminded her that Mercury was about to go retrograde, so this work may not manifest for three weeks to a month. She told me that was okay. This is a very strong and wonderful technique to bring forth your good. Iris had made a "deal" with her Soul. She set a desire and then visualized the outcome.

At the end of the first week, Iris called me back, albeit not too excited, and told me she had just sold her house. I asked her at what price? She said it was for twenty thousand less that her asking price, but the real estate lady had pressured her.

A bit dismayed, I advised her that she had indeed brought up a fabulous Soul lesson for herself. She had not sold her house, but instead, had given into fear and negativity. I

further explained that the sale would not go
through, the people would not be able to get a
mortgage, and that she had to have the patience
to wait until the proper time. All the odds
(energies) were against this free will decision
because:

a) She did not want to sell the house at that
   price
b) She had signed the papers in fear that
   there would not be another buyer
c) It was not a cash sale
d) Mercury was retrograde, confusing the
   decision
e) Natural Law says the deal could not go
   through because she had set a
   previous condition

Another week or so passes, and Iris is
now waiting for the buyers to get their
mortgage, but not me! I was "seeing" a different
picture, and just waiting for Spirit to do its
work.

All this boils down to "I am choosing to
sell my house for a lower price because I have
no patience and believe I want the money rather
than a fair sale." Then you go into denial. The
mind comes up with a coping mechanism. "Oh I
have to do this. There are no other buyers out
there"

The statement she was making was not
true, but we always have to justify our negative
choices. Now what? What happens in your
karmic field with this sort of choice? Well, if
she hadn't set a condition with her Soul prior to

this experience, it could have wound up becoming a disaster. However, Spirit always prevails. The blessing here is the Soul lesson. There is nothing about acquiescing to the fear of the moment that is an expression of our Divinity.

Here's what happened. After three weeks, Mercury moved out of retrograde. Just as that occurred, the buyers were told that they had failed to get a mortgage. The sale became null and void. A few days later, a new buyer came along, anxious to purchase Iris' house, at the asking price, plus one-hundred dollars over, as a cash sale! She happily agreed, but not before the Soul lesson was learned!

Please realize that every choice has its consequences. The positive expression does not get deleted because we are in fear; rather it dwells within the vibration of the Soul and waits for an opening to become expressed. In this case, the Soul was strengthened through the power of two people working together to create a positive, desired outcome.

You may sense that something was wrong, and "see" your own pattern of self-doubt. One keeps manifesting the same situations over and over again, until the Soul can move beyond the negative belief! That's the thing about a negativity that may have happened lifetimes ago. We don't have consciousness about it, but we are sure to continue in the negative pattern until it can be cleared. *Remember, the energy happens before the action!*

By working with Past Life Regression we can become conscious of what choices were made that, in this lifetime, make us feel as if we are banging our head against the wall. This becomes empowering because now we can finally know why our life is the way it is. It is such a gift to realize and understand because we don't have to feel like victims anymore. We can step out into the Light, align with our Soul, and experience the good!

Another example:

Should you continue to try to do good in an organization has become corrupt, or leave and strike out on your own? How can you justify staying, knowing that you're representing a corrupt organization and pretending everyday that it's all good? How does one live with themselves? You begin the denial with "I don't know anything. I'm not as high as they are. They know best. Perhaps it's karma. There must be a good explanation."

You can choose to go against your inner wisdom. To just close down. This will create a huge energy of self-doubt, and you wind up just running around, following anyone who comes along to tell you what to do. No wonder nothing ever works in a life like that.

This action will block you from being aligned and tuning into your own truth anymore. This choice will keep you running after your own tail, but it can be resolved through regression healing work, and by making different decisions in this lifetime.

It can feel empty and scary to leave something so ingrained within you, such as an organization, cult, group, or relationship. It is only after the healing that follows, you realize the truth. Remember the Jim Jones mass suicide? There are many other examples.

By delving into the negative choices we are making, we can find out how that began by going back to the moment of charge, or the original choice that was made in a past life.

When you become aware of your Akashic Records and the choices you made in past-lives, you become incredibly conscious and aware of exactly how we feed our human experience choices. Suddenly, what you attract and why things happen the way they do for you in not a mystery anymore. You get it! This is how you begin to raise your vibration to the higher levels.

These energies are removed and cleared through energetic healing. However, a lot of energetic healing has not been that effective. People keep "slipping back." The secret is to continually change your choices and decisions while going forward without falling back into your comfort zone and old patterns.

New, healthier choices become so much easier when you are no longer burdened by the past. This is your Soul's journey. You understand the nature of the Soul, you understand your Divinity, and then you discover the layers of negativity that are obscuring that Divinity. This prevents you from making choices that attract more negativity and the piling up of more pain and heartache to live through.

We make negative choices, then some positive choices, and life goes on. We may not even know the difference. People begin to make excuses, such as "luck" or "coincidence" to explain the outcome, many of which come from choices made lifetimes ago.

We are 100% in charge of our own experiences. You may not like hearing this at first. We prefer to place the blame outside of ourselves.; this is extremely disempowering and keep you as "the victim." Spiritual empowerment comes from understanding how we create the negativity, learn the ability to clear it, and become *Beings of Light* instead. The beauty is that once you've cleared a lot of this up and begin living in your own Divine nature, you really cannot choose negative choices again because you "get it." You have become aware of who you are. This means that you will no longer make choices based on who you are not.

Your life changes forever because you have stepped into your Divinity. The consciousness you begin to create by walking in your true Divinity, and the choices you will make, will enhance your Spiritual awareness and power. Your life becomes incredible and sometimes uncomfortable. Now that you "know" perhaps you may not want to be that conscious with that much clarity. (Similar to the movie – *"Liar, Liar,"* with Jim Carey)

I will tell you right now that if you don't want to change your life – this work is not for you. Some people don't want to make a change or give up their old behavior. They are still getting something out of it.

This realization changes everything around you forever

It changes your goals

The people around you

The choices that you make

Once you have consciousness, you cannot undo it. You can't unknow something. However, I will tell you this; when we walk in that space of our authentic self expression, we create joy, abundance, fulfillment, balance, and oneness. This is what we are here to experience; our Divine nature, our Soul purpose.

If we don't clear ourselves, then negativity begets negativity, lifetime after lifetime, and we pile up unpleasant experiences and more negative experiences. We become like an onion. These layers and layers of negative blocks obscure our Divinity. This is why we have forgotten our Divine nature completely. This is where most people are these days.

Yes, negativity exists. But remember, we are at cause for everything in our life. We may not like hearing this at first. However, Spiritual empowerment comes from seeing that we create negativity, how to clear it, and how to become a *Being of Light* instead.

ENERGETIC HEALING
SOUL CLEARING

There are a few essential components that must be present for this type of energetic healing, no matter what modality is used. If you are an energy healer of any kind, you will want to learn this information.

When you are working with a client, it would be quite inappropriate to say, "Here is the decision you made many lifetimes ago, and this is why you are experiencing what you are today," and then send them home. People could not cope with that. It is best to begin the clearing work the same day this information is provided.

CLEARING EFFECTIVELY

We bring in our own negativity. We are responsible, which means we get to make a new choice. If we created the negativity then we can clear it. However, responsibility and ownership come first. If we don't face and accept responsibility and ownership, we will literally dis-empower ourselves. We make ourselves victims and then clearing is impossible because you cannot possibly change that which you have no power over.

The most important step to energetically removing negativity is to *take responsibility* for having created it in the first place.

ANOTHER EXAMPLE

One September evening in 1991, I received a call from Donna, a client of mine. She began unveiling a story of horror and deceit that she had been living through for a number of years. The Gypsy neighbor down the hall had gotten hold of her in every way.

Donna admitted that she paid this woman $100,000 over a period of time and that she was out of money and at her wit's end.

I was very saddened and surprised at this news. "Are you willing right now to put an end to this scam and your fear?" I asked.

"Yes, but what can I do," Donna fearfully replied.

"Why are you whispering?"

"I feel that she can hear me," she sobbed.

I explained to Donna that we had to begin *an energetic negativity release* immediately, and although it could take awhile, I was committed to seeing it through. We began the work.

Donna started by saying, *'I am a child of God, I am a child of God,'* over and over, as I instructed.

While Donna was doing that, I began to clear her apartment. Mentally I put myself there and strongly stated, "In the name of God, Christ and the Masters, I order all negative energy to leave now. I order you to leave now!" I asked

Donna to light a white candle and continue declaring that she was and is God's child.

"Put your hand on your solar plexus, and visualize Sharon, the Gypsy woman. Now, I am going to cut the cord that she has attached to your solar plexus. This is how she is gaining power over you. You may be sensitive to this, and Sharon will know that this is happening," I explained as I lit a sandalwood incense stick.

As we were talking, and the conversation lasted more than two hours, there was a knocking, or rather a pounding on Donna's apartment door. The Gypsy woman from down the hall stood outside screaming, "What are you doing? What are you doing?"

"Oh my God, she's at my door," Donna screamed.

"Don't worry and don't answer it. Keep as calm as possible, breathe deeply, and continue working," I replied as calmly as I could.

After about ten minutes, the pounding stopped and Sharon left. We continued working with the energies a little while longer, Donna, claiming to be a child of God, and me, clearing away the entities. It was quite an astral battle.

"Donna, you need to promise you will go to the police and report this first thing in the morning," I said. "It is the only way to keep this protection going. Do not weaken. If you do feel fear, you can call me and I will make myself available to you immediately."

Donna swore that she would. It took almost six months, but Sharon was arrested, convicted, and Donna had most of her money returned to her. Donna worked with the investigating detectives on the Upper East Side of New York City, wore a wire, gathered the evidence, testified in court, and Sharon was convicted. No fees were ever exchanged for my work with Donna. The clearing was pure and came from the heart.

Of course, Sharon's family paid the court costs and fees to lessen her sentence. This is rare that a victim goes to court and actually proves the scam. Donna moved out of New York City and is doing very well now. All the negative energy, from both of their choices, has been removed.

Of course, when we read the Akashic Records and see what choices were made in the past, it may feel easy to say, "Oh, that's how I made that happen. This is why I was weak or keep attracting the same situation over and over again."

The healer's job is to help the client understand what choices they made and help them to see why that created negativity. This is not about beating yourself or you making you wrong. It's not about self-judgment. It's about Spiritual ownership and stepping into your power. This is the first necessary ingredient to effective clearing.

The next ingredient is *consciousness.* You have to know exactly what you are clearing. The more specific we are in naming blocks and restrictions, and the energies we are clearing, the more powerfully focused our intention becomes, and the more powerful the clearing work is.

To clear the "heavy energy blocks" is relatively easy, because that can be done by statements and requests. Many healers try to generally clear energy without having full consciousness of what they are clearing. What is it and how did it get into your life? This is important. If you do not find that answer the result will be very shallow; such as – someone is trying to clear their home or office, but the energy keeps coming back. This does not usually happen. Clearing is done with commands, through intent. Once an area is cleared, it's cleared!

Clearing is only as effective as the amount of consciousness and intent that we bring into the process. Consciousness and setting a condition, setting the intention, must be included in the process. The client as well, must bring their consciousness into the process for the healing to be highly effective.

The healer helps the client to understand the choices that were made in the past that is creating certain consequences now to enable them to understand just how they created what's going on. That's what makes it effective and successful. This is a must for ANY kind of healing modality. Remember, energetic healing work is only as effective as the consciousness of the work.

One has to know the issue, the blocks, the problem before it can be resolved. You are not able to wave the magic wand and say, "Bibbity-Bobbity-Boo," and have a blank slate. That would interfere in the learning process. There would be no Soul lesson.

The whole point of creating and living the life of the Soul; karma, choice, followed by consequences, is perfect. The Divine is teaching us that the consequence informs us of the quality of the choice. Then we use that information to make a different choice next time, hence the growth of the Soul is uplifted to a higher vibration. To circumvent consequences and neglect intention will cancel out the Spiritual Law of Karma.

I know there are hundreds of kinds of energy healing modalities out there that can prove to be highly effective. However you need to claim responsibility for what is going on, for what you are clearing, and you have to bring in full consciousness for what the energy even is. Then the change will come and be recorded into the Akashic Records. Most of all you can change what you attract.

Effective energetic clearing work is like lifting the veil that prevents you from seeing and recognizing the garbage in your life. This garbage of false beliefs clouds our Divinity. After it is lifted, we can see ourselves again. We can step into who we truly are as Divine Beings and we can begin to express our Divinity and Soul level gifts of who we truly are. Once we do that, we begin to create fulfillment and abundance.

Knowing who you are at Soul level and knowing what choices you made that have obscured your Divinity, and then clearing the negative choices so that once again you can be the Divine Light in the world that you've always really been, is a great gift. It truly is worth all the time and effort you spend seeking out this truth.

The clouds have come in, lifetime after lifetime, and you need some window spray and paper towels to wipe them away so that you can see YOU! Then the world will see you as well.

Being able to do that for your clients and family is amazing work. Then you will hear from your loved ones, *"Oh my god, the most amazing shifts are happening. You won't believe the changes that are occurring."* This happens because there is a new energetic flow passing through your body, at a higher vibration rate.

The healing energy of the Akashic Records allows us the freedom to choose *Grace* in all things; therefore, overriding any illusion we have created that causes us to believe we are separate from our Divine Source.

NOTES

NOTES

CHAPTER NINE

Finding Your Soulmate

WIKIPEDIA — *Soul mate (or Soulmate) is a person with whom one has a feeling of deep or natural affinity. This may involve similarity, love, romance, intimacy, sexuality, sexual activity, Spirituality, or compatibility and trust.*

PLATO

In his dialogue *The Symposium*, Plato has Aristophanes present a story about Soulmates. Aristophanes states that humans originally had four arms, four legs, and a single head made of two faces. He continues that there were three genders: man, woman and the

"Androgynous". Each with two sets of genitalia with the Androgynous having both male and female genitalia. The men were children of the sun, the women were children of the earth and the Androgynous were children of the moon, which was born of the sun and earth. It is said that humans had great strength at the time and threatened to conquer the gods. The gods were then faced with the prospect of destroying the humans with lightning as they had done with the Titans, but then they would lose the tributes given to the gods by humans. Zeus developed a creative solution by splitting humans in half as punishment for humanity's pride and doubling the number of humans who would give tribute to the gods. These split humans were in utter misery to the point where they would not eat and would perish so Apollo had sewn them up and reconstituted their bodies with the navel being the only remnant harkening back to their original form. Each human would then only have one set of genitalia and would forever long for his/her other half; the other half of his/her Soul. It is said that when the two find each other, there is an unspoken understanding of one another, that they feel unified and would lie with each other in unity and would know no greater joy than that!

EDGAR CAYCE

According to Theosophy, whose claims were modified by Edgar Cayce, God created androgynous Souls—equally male and female. Later theories postulate that the Souls split into separate genders, perhaps because they incurred karma while playing around on the Earth, and created "separation from God." Over a number of reincarnations, each half seeks the other. When all karmic debt is purged, the two will fuse back together and return to the ultimate.

Some psychologists state that believing that a Soulmate exists specifically for a person is an unrealistic expectation.

#

A Twin Flame (also Twin Soul) is a Spiritual concept describing a special Soul connection between two halves of the same Soul. The Twin Flames are thought to be a template for a new type of relationship between lovers. The fundamental thought behind this concept is that the dawning new era in human Spiritual evolution will be a time when relationships foster enhanced Spiritual growth between lovers, whereas in previous times and still early in the 21st century, couples stay together for purposes of physical survival and economical safety more than anything else.

According to the mythology of Twin Flames, in the beginning of time we were created as a perfect Soul, that was split into two Soul halves — one half female, the other half male; that would then be cast upon Earth to be forever looking for one-another. They would reincarnate over lifetimes with this longing for each other, and once they finally met, they would reunite and be in love and then leave this physical plane as one whole individual Soul.

There are plenty of modernized theories of Twin Flames, many of which present the view that there is a twin flame for everyone (thus confusing catalytic relationships and Soulmates with twin flames) and that the halves of twin flames are not necessarily a male and female, but can also be homosexual Also, some theorists accept that this is not a relationship that can be experienced once in all life cycles only, but repeats over several. However, most take it as a sign of Spiritual enlightenment and a sign of evolution. Despite these differing views, the Twin Flame concept is still very much tied to monogamous ideals, and the thought that only graduate Souls have twin flames on Earth as their purpose is to do Spiritual work and energy work to help the Planet. However, that does not mean a Twin Flame relationship would be something to aspire for. The Soulmates are much more important, due to the mere higher number of Soulmates doing Spiritual work, and a Soulmate relationship is often more harmonious; Twin flames go through a lot of cleansing and purging of the chakras and energetiacal bodies, and with true Twin Flames, the connection is so intense that it causes fear and many twin flames initially run from the experience.

SOULMATES

Soulmates can be lovers, parents, siblings, relatives, best friends and other individuals in our lives who are usually very close to us. As I understand it from my highly evolved teachers, some of who are invisible, four different kinds of Soulmate relationships are possible.

Karmic Soulmates are two individuals who have come together during a given lifetime to heal something from a past life or previous lives. Their relationship with one another can be very profound and loving, or it can deteriorate into the same negative situation that was created in a previous life. Another possible outcome is that the karma may only be partially resolved, leaving both with more work to do during this or some future life together.

All the negative karma we've incurred during any of our previous lives will eventually be healed through decisions that are based upon unconditional love and forgiveness. This will not happen because we are forced to do so as a form of punishment. Rather, our choices to bring healing will be based upon free will, which we and we alone will make.

This is what the Universal Law of Karma is about. Rest be assured, we will have as many lives as we need to eventually balance all we have caused others to feel through fear, anger, hatred, bitterness, jealousy, and other ego-based choices.

The second kind of relationship we can choose to experience with a Soulmate is one that *involves important life lessons.* For example, during our in-between life stay, when the Soul dwells in the ethers of the Soul's vibrationary location, we might plan to have a relationship with another while in physical body that would teach us the value of patience, forgiveness, tolerance, openness, acceptance, honor or another personal behavior that would foster our inner growth and Spiritual awareness. Keep in mind that it could take many lifetimes to appreciate the importance of such qualities, and even more to make them a permanent part of our human nature.

The third type of Soulmate partnership between a man and woman has been generally referred to as a *companion relationship.* These are individuals who join together in a bond of deep love to work on a project together. This might involve the formation of a Spiritual center or the creation of an art gallery, or perhaps the couple will compose music during a prolonged union.

The decision to accomplish a project through this kind of union was made by the two individuals prior to entering the Earth plane. Their choice to do so was arrived at freely, and because both desired the positive energy of the other to enrich their individual Soul growth. This type of partnership may endure for part or all of a lifetime. Having made plans for their coupling prior to entering the Earth plane, the intent may have been for healing karma, for experiencing life lessons that come from partnership, or both. All life-plan contracts, made with Spiritual growth in mind, always override man-made laws or religious dogmas.

The fourth Soulmate relationship we almost always have is a *close friendship* or relationship with a relative. We join such individuals while in physical body simply to enjoy their love, company and energy. Not surprisingly, these individuals have been part of our previous lifetime experiences on many occasions, and are always there for us in a supportive role, throughout this lifetime.

It is very important to keep in mind that all Soulmate relationships help us to remember who we really are, return us to God-centeredness and prepare us Spiritually for the eventual reunion with our twin Soul. As such, they can be extremely valuable and should be honored and respected for these very blessed reasons.

A dramatically different kind of relationship exists that is considered to be the most profound and compelling of all. This is the *tein Soulor* or *twin flame union* that will eventually transcend all others. However, because it is so highly charged with energy, the two individuals must be Spiritually ready for the relationship to last any meaningful length of time. When fully prepared, this union is meant to endure for eternity, because of its relationship to the ultimate Oneness we will all seek with Divine Source.

It is important to realize that any relationship you may now be having, whether it be Soulmate, twin-Soul or not, has the potential to be a glorious, fulfilling, extremely loving and very rewarding one, assuming that is what both individuals are striving for.

The coming together of twin Souls does not guarantee fulfillment any more than a Soulmate relationship might bring. What increases the chance for lasting twin reunion is that both twin Souls must be Spiritually prepared for their relationship and then constantly find ways to make it work on that basis. The key ingredient is unconditional, unselfish love and the desire to base the union on a Spiritual rather than an ego-based foundation. Only Spiritually mature couples can deal with the influence of the ego in relationships, which is the major reason for their success.

Always remind yourself that all relationships have a higher purpose. They create and bring balance to the life. God created relationships to inspire us to understand and remember who we really are. Relationships constantly have to be adjusted, accepted, and worked on. After all, if you had no one to relate to, how could you know yourself? That is why all relationships are *sacred*.

THE DIFFERENT TYPES OF SOULMATES

Many of us grow up counting on a fairytale romance, where love magically happens without effort. Sometimes we just coast along wishing and hoping for that illusionary happy ending. While it is healthy to believe in the miracles and magic of love, it is also necessary to be practical and proactive in creating your own romantic destiny. The search for true love is a lot smoother and healthier if you know exactly what you seek in a relationship. Once you have this clarity, you can literally put a casting call out to the Universe for your fabulous co-star!

This visualization exercise is a Soulmate Project in which you use your Third Eye, intellect, emotions and Spirit to clarify and put forth your intentions for love. In this uplifting and supportive technique, you will be carefully guided to construct your personal *Romantic Request Vision Board* based on your Soul's desire for true and lasting love. You will also learn many Spiritual tools to draw in your Soulmate. This is an approach probably unlike any other you've tried to date but worth every ounce of effort and energy. This exercise is best done on a New Moon.

CREATE A SOUL MATE VISION BOARD

Get a piece of cardboard or white poster board, scotch tape, and lots of magazines. Many people, including the very rich ones, use this visualization technique to manifest their desires. On the New Moon, every month, create your personal vision board.

Find a piece of poster board, white if possible, about 8 x 10 and get out your scotch tape. Then find some magazines or go on-line to print out your graphics. You must not use your handwriting, so you have to find the printed words to describe your Soulmate and the qualities you wish them to have. Also find a picture of someone who may look like your Soulmate, including height, hair color, eye color, etc. Be sure to get as specific as you can.

After you have completed the board, stare at it for about five minutes a day— everyday! Create a mantra to think while you are staring at the vision board. What you are doing is taking the vision of your desire inside, where it will manifest.

As Louise Hay teaches us, *"Whatever you visualize, you actualize."* Try it and you will find that it works!

Soulmates are friends and loved ones who are responsive to your love, and with whom you are deeply connected and share a common vibration, path and purpose. Your Soulmate may be someone who has come to be with you and learn similar lessons. A Soulmate can also be someone who has come to assist you in your Spiritual growth by showing you more about yourself and offering you ways to open your heart. I will call these people Soulmates, because this was my role as an identical twin, and I am very familiar with it.

A Soulmate can be someone who is connected to you from other lifetimes and with whom you are continuing a well-developed past-life relationship. Or, this may be your first lifetime together on earth, as was the case with my twin and I.

Most people have more than one Soulmate. You may already be in several Soulmate relationships with friends and loved ones. A Soulmate can come in the form of a life partner, treasured friend, parent, relative, sibling, child, or lover. A Soulmate can be someone with whom you share a Spiritual path, to do joint work in the world, or it may be a commitment to be parents to certain Souls. It can be someone whose growth you are sponsoring, such as a sibling or a foster child. Soulmates can be an older, younger, or the same-age Soul. Soul age is the amount of Soul love, Soul will and purpose, and Soul Light that people are able to express through their personalities.

Soul age reflects the degree to which people are living as Souls and the receptivity of their personalities to their Souls. The age of a Soul in the examples that follow is relative. You may be a very old Soul, and a Soul you are with may also be a very old Soul, yet a younger Soul than you are. Or, you may be with an older Soul than you are, yet still be an old Soul yourself. If you want to attract a Soulmate for an intimate relationship, decide if you want to attract a younger, same-age, or older Soul as your Soulmate. Or, you can leave the choice up to your Blessed Higher Self, guides, and Soul.

Being in an intimate relationship with a younger Soul offers you many opportunities to develop the qualities of teaching, serving, and empowering. Younger Souls can offer you the chance to pass on much of what you have learned, and to recognize the growth you have gained. Being a teacher can be very rewarding when the younger Soul is willing to grow and wants to learn from you. If the younger Soul does not want to change or grow, you will most likely feel drained and frustrated rather than energized. If someone's Soul age is a great deal younger than yours, you may expend much energy with few results. This is known as a vibrational span and can interfere with the harmony and balance in your life.

In a relationship with a younger Soul, you will have an opportunity to gain the Soul qualities of patience and compassion. You will learn how to empower others without taking responsibility for their lives, saving them, or taking away their lessons. You will discover how to be in a relationship with someone whose vision is not as expanded or as farseeing as yours. You will be challenged to be loving, humble, forgiving, and kind. Younger Souls sometimes feel threatened by older Souls, and may try to reduce an older Soul's confidence and personal power to feel better about themselves. This is called sharpening their ego, and brings discouragement and negativity, which can erode both Souls.

If you decide to join with a younger Soul, be certain that this person wants what you have to offer and is receptive to change and growth. When this is the case, you can find it very rewarding to be with a younger Soul and watch this person evolve.

Most personalities choose to be in relationships with Souls who are of a similar Soul age to yourself. With a same-age Soul, you will often be growing at the same rate, and learning some of the same lessons. There is the potential for great joy as well as for intense conflicts in a same-age Soul relationship.

You will be challenged to gain the Soul qualities of self-love. The degree to which you love yourself will determine your ability to love the other person, who will be reflecting back to you many of your own personality traits and qualities, some of which you may not like. A same-age Soul relationship has the potential of being very intimate, for knowing the other can be like knowing yourself. You will need to be vulnerable and allow another person into your heart. You will begin to love what you have considered unlovable in yourself as a part of loving the other person. You will gain by letting go of blame and self-pity, and by recognizing that you can only receive from the other person what you can give to yourself. You will be challenged to control and work with your emotions and to know where you end and the other person begins. Setting boundaries are very important in such a relationship.

Being in a relationship with an older Soul brings different kinds of challenges. You might think that relationships with older Souls would be the easiest, because of the compassion, understanding, and Spiritual Light they can offer you. *With an older Soul, you will be the student.* You will be challenged to grow and to let go of any unevolved solar plexus ego reactions. If the Soul you are with is too advanced, you may be called to grow at a pace that is too rapid for you. In this relationship you will have an opportunity to learn how to love yourself without judging, comparing yourself, or feeling unworthy or inferior.

Older Souls are often able to detach from personality reactions, offering you a more impersonal, wiser love. This might not always be comfortable to you. The gifts an older Soul gives may come in different forms than what you want, so you will need to focus on the essence of what you receive rather than on your expectations of certain actions, words, or behaviors. You will be with someone whose vision is more farseeing than yours, so you will need to learn to trust in yourself and develop your own inner vision. You will need to learn when to surrender to the wisdom and guidance of the other person, and when to be your own authority.

An older Soul can offer much in a relationship, and can be a delight to be with. Older Souls can teach you many things. They can make many valuable contributions to your life with their wisdom, insight, and perspectives. They can assist you in growing through the example of the way they live and think about their lives. As in any relationship, a relationship with an older Soul has many rewards, as well as many challenges. You will learn to let go of thinking your Soulmate will fulfill your every expectation as well as become more self-responsible. Openness and honesty will be a critical part of this relationship.

PREPARING TO JOIN WITH YOUR SOULMATE

If you want to attract a life partner as your Soulmate, there are several illusions you will need to relinquish first. One is that your Soulmate is someone you will be with for the rest of your life. You can have a Soulmate relationship that lasts a few weeks, months, or years. Time has nothing to do with the quality of your connection and its importance in your life. You may be in a Soulmate relationship with someone that lasts for the rest of your life, or you may have learned all you came together to learn and fulfilled the higher purposes of your relationship in just a few months or years. Do not measure the quality or importance of a relationship based on the length of time you are together.

Another illusion is that there is only one Soulmate who is your true life partner. You may have already had a Soulmate connection with a life partner, sharing a caring loving bond that created much growth for you. Just because your outer connection has ended does not mean that this was not a Soulmate relationship. There are several Soulmates who could be right for you, if it is indeed time for you to have a Soulmate in your life. Who you attract at any given time will depend upon the lessons you need to learn and the higher path you are choosing. It will also depend on your Soulmate's readiness to be with you.

In any Soulmate relationship, you will need to let go of the illusion that there is a perfect person waiting for you who will fulfill your every expectation and give your personality everything it desires once you are together. Do not expect your ideal Soulmate to be someone who is always loving and easy to get along with, who agrees with everything you say or do, and who brings you a life of ease and comfort. You may experience your Soulmate in this way at times, and at other times this person may challenge you to love as your Soul does through his or her unevolved, but very human, expressions of love.

Soulmates always bring you growth and give you many chances to awaken your heart centers. Sometimes this process of growth is easy, and sometimes it is not. Soulmate relationships offer you wonderful opportunities to work at the Soul level.

Remember, the term Soulmate means many different things. These are Souls that you have experienced and shared with in past or parallel lifetimes. They can also be other aspects of your Soul, experiencing life at this time in another body. We are all multidimensional beings, your Soul may be having experiences in many realities and dimensions, at the same time. As we all evolve from the same Divine source of consciousness creation, we could say that we are all Soulmates in a manner of speaking. This is what the Oneness is all about. *What you do to me you also do to yourself.*

In summary, the word Soulmate is sometimes used to designate someone with whom one has a feeling of deep and natural affinity, friendship, love, intimacy, sexuality, and/or compatibility. Soulmates can have various types of relationships, which do not always include romantic love. They can be close friends, co-workers, a teacher, anyone who influences your life one way or another. They can play the emotional, Spiritual, physical, and mental, games of third dimension with you. They can affect relationships in a positive or negative way depending on the emotional issues of the people concerned.

REVIEW

- Souls often come together to work out issues or play reverse roles than that which they are experiencing elsewhere.

- Anyone who is in your biological family, or adopted family, or pseudo-family, is a Soulmate to you.

- You feel closer to certain Souls, because you have attracted them into your life as they are on the same frequency as you or because you want to work out issues with them.

- Karma refers to contracts and responsibilities shared by Soulmates.

- Often Soulsmates come together to bring another Soul into the physical realms. A man and woman mate and produce one or more children, the karma thus completed ends. The couples separate and share whatever karma is linked to the child.

- Sometimes the karma in a family is between mother and child, so the child remains exclusively with the mother. Sometimes the karma is with the father and the mother leaves or deceases. Sometimes it is with both parents or with a sibling who has entered the family before or after you.

LONGING FOR ROMANCE

As the Soul seeks unity with the Self, (a twin flame connection), it tends to think of a Soulmate as The One (which is actually the Divine Source of creation) who is there for us and to make us feel complete.

Did you know that you often attract people into your life who look as you did in past lives? For example, you are a man seeking a female partner, you will seek out someone who looks and acts as you would if you were a woman, like your mirror image. Your ideal partner is who you were in that physical body. We are always seeking new ways to experience ourselves.

Soulmates express and can bring out the best and worst in each other, depending on their issues, and often no matter how hard someone tries to hold on and help, when it's time for them to leave our lives, *the lesson is to let go.*

ARE YOU READY TO MEET YOUR SOULMATE?

- Are you stuck in a love rut?

- Finding yourself yearning for that special someone?

- Having a tough time meeting the "right" person?

- Pondering questions like, how to find true love and how do I find my Soulmate?

- Frustrated by chronic patterns that repeat themselves over and over again in relationships? The same energy in a different face?

- Do you feel ready—truly ready—to meet your Soulmate? A balanced partner? The mirror image of you?

In the new energy of the New Earth in the Twenty-First Century, we are beginning to connect with our Soulmates. Soulmate unions are about acceptance, self-love, patience and honesty. *Your heart needs to be open and you need to have found peace about yourself within yourself.* Soulmates accept one another for who and what they are without question or judgment.

So, who is this special ONE that we want to share our lives with? In his book, *Only Love Is Real*, Brian Weiss's description is this:

"There is someone special for everyone. Often there are two or three, or even four. They come from different generations. They travel across oceans of time and the depths of heavenly dimensions to be with you again. They come from the other side, from heaven. They look different, but your heart knows them. You are bonded together throughout eternity and you will never be alone."

Rumi also said it thousands of years ago, *"True lovers don't meet somewhere, they're in each other all along."*

Soulmate unions are about acceptance, self-love, patience, and honesty. It is necessary to ask for guidance from your Blessed Higher Self, Spirit Guides and Angels to guide you in the direction needed for the highest good for all concerned when seeking a Soulmate.

Self-love is the ultimate giving to the Self, meaning that you are completely honest within yourself about what you are doing in all areas of your life. Are you with the partner that you love, and is that love appreciated, or do you give of yourself so much and receive minimal back. If this describes you and you are still in that relationship, then you are in a Third Dimensional relationship, and perhaps you are not being honest with yourself.

Stand back and look at yourself from an objective viewpoint and be totally honest about how you feel in your heart about where you belong. Your heart will only be clear when you have worked through all your issues and attained a space of peace within, and this includes the practice of self love.

From self love comes *walking your talk*. Do you have enough courage to love yourself enough to be able to make changes in your life that ultimately give to yourself the peace of mind and the life that you want? If not, then it is time to take a good, long look at yourself.

Your physical condition is a good sign of the Spiritual counterpart. Sometimes your body parts scream Spiritual messages to you, loud and clear.

From: *You Can Heal Your Life* by Louise Hay

If your eyes cannot focus near- what is it in your life that you cannot focus on, and it will be on the things of the now that are happening in your life.

If you cannot focus far- then you have no vision of your future.

If you are overweight- what is it that you are holding on to; what are you protecting yourself from?

A pain in the neck/back is what or who in your life is a pain in the neck and who are you carrying?

A pain in the heart- who in your life is causing heartbreak?

Blistered or sore feet-are you having difficulty in walking your path?

Bladder infections-who or what in your life is making you pissed off?

Vaginal infections/irritations-look at your sexual relationships and the emotional attachments behind them.

Problems with throat infections, phlegm-what truth needs to be spoken by you?

Bad breath or mouth problems-look and see how you are speaking to others?

Ears-what is it in your life that you are not listening to? (Inner guidance).

Hungry-what is it in your life that you crave? True love?

It is always good to follow your inner guidance, and to feed it with positive affirmations.

HOW TO RECOGNIZE YOUR SOULMATE;

Recognizing a Soulmate comes in many forms and ways. If you are not ready it simply will not be happen to you. Often meeting a Soulmate causes a Spiritual awakening that has its own difficulties to deal with. On a vibrational level you will feel an immense connection and compatability, as if you can never be apart again.

You will be attracted to one another with a deep magnetic attraction or wanting to merge with this person. You will be sexually attracted to one another.

You need to be in close physical contact for this and this union is not a planned event; it is an event based on Divine timing or synchronicity such as an eye gaze, handshake, or hug.

On a Spiritual level, the Third Eye opens fully in both of you and you scan one another for the matching and harmonizing Light vibrational frequency. If you are indeed a match, then the higher selves will immediately communicate to you that it is a "perfect fit," or "future wife/husband," or "Soulmate". You may have had visions of joining with this person before the first meeting.

If you are clairvoyant then you will more than likely begin a Spiritual relationship with one another that is comfortable and rewarding. Your Soulmate may bring you roses every day, communicate to you in meditations, telepathy, and wrap their energy around you in support.

The roses are to help you open the heart. On a Spiritual level it is a joy and a gift to have this communication between you. This may be difficult for you, because the Third Dimensional relationship is different and not on the same level of honesty and truth as the Spiritual one. It is up to you as to how you wish to accept the things to come and how difficult you choose to make this relationship for yourself.

It may be best to stand back and request higher guidance; the time will come when you will connect and when you do you will know. Trust your heart, and know that it will guide you well.

This joining, a unity of love between two entities, is the meaning of SOULMATES.

#

To Spiritually connect with your Soulmate continue to the meditation.

MEDITATION FOR SOULMATES
FOR PHYSICAL AND SPIRITUAL UNION

Surround yourself with White Light, close your eyes and center yourself.

Ask your Blessed Higher Self, Guides, and Angels to come in and guide you. Take yourself into your sacred heart space, and feel the brilliant color of yellow, amber. The sacred heart space of the Soulmates is divided in two, half yours and half your partner's. This exercise/meditation will give you a clear indication of where you are at any particular time, and will give you much needed advice and comfort when needed.

Imagine yourself at the Lake in your calm scene. You are standing in the arc rays of White Light, this sacred arc is in the middle of a meadow. You will see a forest at the edge of the meadow. Call your Soulmate, ask them to walk out of the forest and into your life now and to make themselves known to you.

Ask you Soulmate to meet you there in the meadow, and connect with you. If you cannot see anything do not worry. The intent to connect is what is needed. Take a long, good look at the figure approaching you. Notice their appearance, their walk, their ambiance. Then take the time to set the conditions of the character you wish them to have. Make bold, positive statements. You can repeat the qualities you have on your vision board.

Have a telepathic conversation with your Soulmate. Tell your Soulmate anything you wish, for this is a precious connection time and it is sacred and honored by both of you. Send and receive Love to one another in this sacred space. Take your time and allow the energy to flow, and then clear. You will "know" when the meditation is over.

If you cannot see, then just tune into the warmth present and set the intent/condition to feel the Love.

You may wish to give or receive something from one another. It could be a symbol or a word or a feeling. Stay in this space as long as you like.

#

Write this experience down! Take notes as soon as you can compose yourself after the meditation, so you do not forget, and are able to refer to them at any later date.

NOTES

CHAPTER TEN

How Do I Manifest

As you enter the Fifth Dimension you may come to the frightening conclusion that you are the decisive element in your life. It is your personal approach that creates the climate. It is your daily mood that makes the weather. You possess tremendous power to make life miserable or joyous. Everything or anything you want, whether it is more money, better health, a house of your own, or just to be happy; is already inside of you. All the things that you currently see and experience as reality are simply a symptom of what is happening inside of you. You have learned that when you change what is on the inside and you automatically change what is on the outside.

What you experience today is a result of what you created yesterday and the day before. Unless you change something inside of you today, tomorrow will continue the same way that yesterday and the day before have been. But how do you create the new reality you want as opposed to the current reality that you don't want? How can you bring about the necessary changes to improve your life?

You do this by focusing only on the new reality that you want. This may be difficult to do when you have bills overdue with no money in the bank and creditors calling you everyday.

First Step —

Meditate-work your Chakras and Spiritual Chakras (8 to 9) and relax:

Get clear of any opposing negative energy. There are specific exercises you can do and steps you can take, which are at the back of the book. The Sat Nam, Breath of Fire, Ring of Fire, work your Chakras and then wrap in White Light.

Focus on the things you really want, feel rejuvenated and refreshed, gain perspective on what you need to do to change your situation for good.

How Do I Manifest?

There is one question that has always been asked, and it is "How do I manifest?" And the answers always went something like the following:

(1) Visualize repeatedly, see yourself having or doing whatever it is you wish to manifest before you actually get it.

(2) Affirm or repeat statements or thoughts that are consistent with your desire. Continually affirm that you have already received your desire.

(3) Write down all your desires in a notebook as if you have already received it.

(4) Be grateful for what you already have, by expressing gratitude to the Divine.

Now you may be doubtful that you can achieve any results while wondering, is this true. Will I really manifest my desires if I do the above?

The answer is a categorical *Yes,* especially if you add the Circle of Light techniques and energy. But why is it then that people keep asking that question, *how do I manifest?* Why are people unable to manifest their desires and dreams, even though the answer is given to them over and over?

Here is the problem

Your mind is a creature of habit, it likes the familiar; for most people this would mean, repeated failure and a constant struggle. When you affirm something else, for example, "I am rich beyond my wildest dreams," your mind will

191

resist this new information because it doesn't match what the mind and emotions are used to. It takes time to process the new message through your cellular memory. It's kind of like hypnosis and affirmations. These techniques work because of the repetition. (Kind of like etheric hypnosis)

That's why you'll find that whenever you try to think a positive thought there will be a fleeting negative thought that will create doubt in your mind and will over-ride your positive thought. What happens is that even though you have learned how to direct your power and manifest what you want, your conscious mind resists, and prevents this new life-changing information from impressing upon your *subconscious*, and super-conscious minds, which is the energy that attracts all your experiences.

Even though you consciously try to visualize and affirm a new reality you are still going to experience negative events from time to time. For most people this would be a confirmation of discouragement causing the thought that "affirmations" and "visualization" doesn't work. So they get distracted and return to their old way of thinking, talking and behaving. Unfortunately this means that they will keep on attracting the same old responses, which includes fear of poverty, things going wrong, and frustration.

Positive Thinking

The key to manifesting your desires is to affirm and visualize them with positive emotion and to be consistent and unrelenting with the daily visualization, irrespective of whether you see change or not; over a period of time you will bring about a different reality. When that happens you will no longer have to ask, *how do I manifest*, because you'll see your life being transformed before your very eyes.

It is believed that all of us on this earth have a calling. It is taught in many religious sectors and society, that we were sent here to accomplish a specific task. But if you don't know what you were meant to do, can you still manifest your destiny? Probably not.

The first thing you need to figure out then is what you were meant to do this lifetime on this planet. I think a good way to find this out is to discover what your passion is. This is because your passion is closely connected to your purpose. Many successful people don't think even think much about what they were meant to do, they just follow their passion and everything falls into place.

Find your Soul Destiny

Find out what you're good at.

What is the thing that most people complement you on?

When are you the happiest? What is the one activity that makes you smile and forget about your troubles?

Your life's purpose will always affect other people around you in a positive way. Go within and decide on what direction you want to go in. Most of the time the blockage is not because you don't know what your destiny is. You know what you want to be, and what you need to do, but you're scared of failing or making a fool of yourself. So *fear* keeps you rooted in one place, year after year.

Heads up—time to learn something new. Remember, If you don't do anything, then nothing will happen, period. The only way you'll get to manifest your destiny is if you make a quality decision and start moving on it. As soon as you do that you'll find that magic starts to happen for you. This is what is called *taking a quantum leap!*

You simply cannot skirt the issue. Do you wake up every morning knowing—with every fiber of your Soul—that you're enjoying the most creative life you can make for yourself?

* Do you love your work?

* Do you spend enough time with the family?

* Are you earning enough?

* Are you putting your creativity potential to full use?

* Are you as healthy as you should be?

* Are you truly happy?

99% of people would say "No!" This is no surprise. We've all got pain, issues, and upset in our lives that need fixing, whether they're professional, personal, or health-related. Issues that we just can't seem to iron out, no matter where, how, or who we look too. In fact, sometimes we've searched so much for the answer that we begin to wonder whether it really exists anywhere on this planet! Here's the thing – *sometimes, it doesn't*.

That's where connection to the Divine comes in. Why? Because this process to manifesting your desires, connecting to the Fifth Dimension energies, brings you both the foundations of personal success, along with love, peace, and harmony in your life, world, and the planet.

The Fifth Dimension connection helps you:

*Attract wealth and abundance

*Instantly boost creativity and pick up new skills like painting, photography, and singing

*Manifest your destiny and always know what decision to make when faced with multiple options

*Find inspiration, wisdom and knowledge in every situation

*MANIFEST everything you DESIRE that is in alignment with your Soul's destiny.

That secret is a technique called *Quantum Jumping*.

"What On Earth Is Quantum Jumping?" you ask.

Quantum Jumping is the process of "jumping" into parallel dimensions, and gaining creativity, knowledge, wisdom and inspiration from alternate versions of yourself—both from past lives, parallel lives, and future lives.

Are you still with me? Does that sound crazy? It did to me at first—which is precisely why this information has been held back until it's the right time, a time when mankind would be willing and able to open their mind to this new way of living and Soul expression.

And that time is now. Why? Because some of the finest minds on the planet are starting to discover evidence supporting the Fifth Dimension energies; creative and scientific geniuses like Stephen Hawking, Michio Kaku, and Neil Turok, all of whom are responsible for unbelievable breakthroughs in the field of quantum physics.

But just as important as the acknowledgement of experts is what I've seen and experienced for myself. After sharing Quantum Jumping with others, I've seen this process manifest incredible results. There are stories of creativity and inspiration, stories of rags to riches, the kind of stories you'd usually only find in those feel good Hollywood blockbuster movies.

And now it's time for you to create your own story—so that you, and as many people as possible, can gain an understanding of this remarkable phenomenon, and change your life for the better. You're can experience Quantum

Jumping for yourself. The Quantum Jumping experience will teach you.

    * How to perform your very own Quantum Jump. And no, you don't need any sort of mental or psychic talent.

    * Why Quantum Jumping is the key to manifesting a better you.

    * What the scientists are saying. Need proof? I don't blame you— the proof is in your own personal experience.

Once you've gone through this deep meditation on manifesting for yourself, within the Circle of Light, you'll have a firm understanding of Quantum Jumping, what it can do, and how it's going to change your life.

You are not a physical being in a physical Universe. You are an energetic/vibrational being in an energetic/vibrating Universe. You are both a transmitter and a receiver of energy. One of your greatest challenges as a human being is learning how to live as a vibrational being in a vibrating Universe. It seem almost like defying the Laws of Physics.

Attracting Compatible Patterns

When you don't attract into your life what you want, you still are attracting what you are thinking about. You may not attract what you feel or desire. Desires, thoughts, and feelings are all important, but these are more effects than causes. You attract from your sub-conscious memory field, past-life memories, and karmic holdings, and that's what needs to change, or be reprogrammed. It used to be complicated and time consuming, but now it's instantaneous with the power of *setting conditions*.

You attract what you're signaling

Think of yourself as a vibrational transmitter. You're constantly sending out signals that tell the Universe who you are in this moment. Those signals will either attract or repel other vibrational beings, events, and experiences both into and out of your life.

You naturally attract that which is in harmony with your current *vibrational rate*, and you'll repel that which is out of sync with your level or vibration, for good or for ill.

If your energetic self radiates wealth and abundance, your physical reality will reflect wealth and abundance for your physical being. If your energetic self radiates anger and frustration, your physical reality will reflect that as well.

Since the signals you're sending out at any given moment tend to be fairly complex, your experience of physical reality will be equally complex. Once you can accept that your vibrational self attracts compatible patterns, it becomes clear that if you want to experience something different in your life, you must somehow change the signals, almost like radio signals, and vibrations you're putting out.

Your Vibrational Hum

Listen to the vibrational hum of your being. Quiet your mind, tune into your inner being, and listen to the ever-broadcasting radio station that is you. What types of signals are you broadcasting in this moment?

When I tune in to my Inner Helper for a moment, I can sense some of the signals that are emanating from me. I can feel that I'm radiating happiness and joy. I can sense that I'm sending out signals to attract positive, loving, new relationships into my life. I can sense that I'm radiating financial abundance and increase. I can sense when my energy is very mental at any moment.

These are all thoughts, however. The true signal I'm emitting isn't a thought. It's a *frequency*. I might describe this frequency in words, but I can never get the words quite right because human language is inadequate to the task. In spite of this, if I try to describe my current signal, I might use the following adjectives: flowing, smiling, happy, peaceful, soaring, white, soft, strong, expanding, warm, mindful, smooth, and energized.

I can also tune into signals from my environment. I can sense that my belly is broadcasting satiety after a meal. I can observe that it's 59 degrees F outside. I can hear soft music coming from computer speakers (sound is yet another vibration). I can subtly perceive sounds from a TV signal transmitting from the next room. I can feel the combined energy of the people around the world.

Overall, I can sense if the signals I'm sending out and the signals coming from my environment are in sync. I feel happy, peaceful, and abundant, and my environment reflects that. This is a safe, stable state, and one I experience often.

Your *energy signature* is the summation of all the signals you're sending out. Your thoughts and feelings aren't the cause of these signals though; your thoughts and feelings are actually effects of the signals. If you change the signal you're emitting, your thoughts and feelings will shift as well. This is how we change our minds, or fall in and out of love. It all depends on what we are currently vibrating to.

Vibrational Equilibrium

Your vibrational being and your environment will tend to move toward its individual equilibrium over time. If your current life situation appears fairly stable, it's safe to say that you're maintaining equilibrium.

For example, if you're financially broke, and if this is a stable situation that has persisted for some time, then it's likely that most of the energetic signals you're exposing yourself to are also vibrating at a similar frequency of brokeness. This includes the place you live, the people you interact with, your work environment, events on your calendar, your furniture, and so on. Your being is immersed in a field of these signals, and this encourages you to vibrate at the same level.

If you continue to surround yourself with signals that reinforce your current state, then that state will persist indefinitely. You may be able to get away from it for a while, but you'll keep coming back to it, if that's your equilibrium.

Shifting Your Vibration

Creating a temporary shift in your vibration is easy. You can create such a change in seconds. Jump around and move your body. Sing your favorite song. Smile for a minute. Hold a yoga pose. Take a cold shower. All of these will help to change your emotional and vibrational state. However, this won't create any sort of lasting change if you return to your old vibration afterwards. If your dominant inner signal remains unchanged, your equilibrium won't shift. In order to shift your equilibrium, you need to break free from creating the old equilibrium. This means you must create a lasting disconnect between your current vibration and the environmental vibrations that are compatible with it in order to grow and create a new vibration.

There are basically two ways to change vibrations

First, you can learn how to shift your own vibration long enough to create a lasting disconnect with your current environment. If you start transmitting with a new signal, you'll soon repel whatever in your environment is incompatible with your new signal. You'll also begin attracting other people, events, and experiences that are compatible with your new signal. Hold the new vibration long enough, and you'll see your whole physical reality change all around you.

You can apply this approach by visualizing your goals within the Circle of Light vividly *for at least 20 minutes per day.* Visualize in such a way that you will begin to feel strong emotions of the visualization becoming your inner reality. An emotional shift from within indicates that you're broadcasting a new signal. The longer you can hold this new vibration, the faster your reality will shift. (Do the exercise preferably before bedtime so that you can work on it for a subconscious state while sleeping, and without conscious thought.)

The second method is to intentionally replace many of your environmental signals with new ones. *Then you must hold yourself in that new environment.* (For example, change you behavior response. Many of us do this, temporarily, after a Spiritual Retreat.) This will feel uncomfortable at first because you won't initially be compatible with those new signals. You must allow them to recalibrate your own vibration until you become compatible with them.

You can also apply this approach by changing your environmental landscape— physically, socially, and otherwise. For example, stop spending time with your lazy friends, give away your TV, stop all those computer games, and hang out every day with the most productive people you know. Changing your habits will feel uncomfortable at first, but eventually you'll start to integrate those new signals, and your own vibrational pattern will soon shift to come into resonance with these new people.

To sum up, you can either change the signal you're emitting, or you can change the signal level you're immersed in. *Either way can be very effective at creating a lasting change in your vibrational pattern.*

Creating What You Desire

To create what you want in your life, you must shift up your vibrational pattern such that you're emitting a signal that's vibrationally compatible with your goals and desires.

You can identify that new vibration by vividly visualizing your goals until you feel different emotions, and those emotions stabilize at a certain point. Notice how your vibrational inner being feels, not just emotionally but energetically as you visualize your good. Then return to your old state, and notice the vibrational difference between the two states. Compare and contrast the old vibration with the new one.

For example, here's how I'd describe the vibration of being broke and deep in debt, a frequency I emitted for many years: tight, knotted, twisted, chaotic, rough, blurry, red, dark, fast, changing, pressed, and squeezed.

Here's how I'd describe the vibration of financial abundance: open, free, clear, bluish-white, flowing, smooth, green, bright, focused, and intense.

Each vibration has a different energy signature. If I temporarily shift my default vibration to a state of feeling broke (just by imagining it as real or verbalizing the belief), I can feel my vibrational self shifting its frequency too. If I held that vibration long enough, I'd soon find that my physical reality followed suit.

Hopefully it's obvious by now that if you want to shift your vibration, it's a bad idea to consistently expose yourself to incompatible signals, or continue shopping with all those credit cards. Watch the TV news about the ongoing financial meltdown and the recession/depression, and notice what happens to your vibration. Then notice what happens to your finances in the long run. If you want to experience financial abundance, this is a very bad time to watch or read mainstream news. This is the perfect time to read high-quality books or articles instead.

Learning to sense and control the vibrational frequencies you're emitting is powerful stuff. Once you really get this, you can intentionally shift your frequency at will to experience what you desire.

If you want to experience wealth, you can create that. If you want to experience a new relationship, you can create that too. If you want to be debt free, you can create it. If you want high energy and good health, you can create that as well.

This isn't to say that it will be easy for you to accomplish all of these things. It takes practice to adjust your vibrational frequency correctly, so be patient with yourself. Remember—Rome wasn't manifested in a day.

One more thing: *You cannot receive that which you cannot give to yourself.*

#

How to Manifest Your Dreams and Desires

Now that we have begun to experience the energetic gifts of 2012, for many, it is time to evaluate their life and *set new conditions* to help bring about new, positive change. This is a very healthy process and, if done correctly, can be instrumental in helping you uplift your life and bring about the changes you desire and dream about.

Dr. Deepak Chopra has often pointed out the power of the mind when it comes to manifesting your desires and creating the reality you wish for. In addition, what I would like to do is give you a very practical visualization technique to help you manifest these desires that you have settled upon.

There are many powerful visualization techniques and visualization meditations which you can use to help you create your reality, and the one below is one of the simplest, yet most effective techniques out of all these.

Simple Visualization Technique to Manifest Your Desires:

Write down your desires and goals on a piece of paper and keep it handy for review, first thing in the morning, as much as possible throughout the day, and *last thing at night*. That's the core aspect of this technique. Bring your thoughts and images inside, so they can begin to magnetize outward. This visualization technique has many advantages. (3 x 5 file cards are still in vogue for this exercise.)

1. Clarify Your Desires and Help Yourself Visualize:

In having to contemplate and write down your desires, you will have to spend some time digging into them more deeply. This process is very helpful in helping you see exactly what it is that you want, as well as guiding you to stop all of the negative behavior that you don't want. By having to think about it, articulate it, and write it down, helps you further refine and define the desire, thus giving the mind a very clear picture of what it needs to manifest for you. That is correct. Once the mind knows and sees what it is that you want, it will help make that dream a reality. It does this because that's Natural Law; *We actualize what we visualize.*

2. Enforce Your Desires and Give Yourself Willpower:

Writing down your desires and keeping them handy for review, helps re-enforce inside what it is you want to accomplish. This will serve as a constant reminder to you as you go through your day and help you make choices that promote the accomplishment of these goals. This technique is very handy in helping you prioritize your tasks and gives you the willpower to overcome past habits, obstacles and pitfalls. In addition, the mind, being well aware of what it is that you are looking to realize, will work with life to help you.

3. Help You Stick to It:

That piece of paper or file card will not only serve as a daily reminder, but it will also help keep you on track after the initial passion starts to wane, and believe me, it will.

4. Allow the Mind to Meditate and Contemplate the Desires:

Without making it an obsession, reviewing your desires from time to time gives the mind a chance to contemplate and visualize what it is that your are looking to manifest. Contemplation and meditation on the desires are key in sending a clear message to your mind about what it is that you wish to have manifest in your life. I suggest you review and write a new *message of desire* to the Universe on every New Moon.

Example of My List of Desires:

Here is the list of goals and desires I put together some time ago. The list is to help serve as an example for you.

> 1. Establish a strong personal Spiritual practice.

> 2. Have excellent and vibrant health.

3. Enjoy a happy relationship with my family and friends.

4. Continue to develop my TV writing ability and align my career with it more.

5. Write a book – a best seller!

6. Work with Ignite to create new residual income.

7. Have the freedom and courage to live my true life.

Final Thoughts:

All that you have ever wanted and more is already inside of you. How to manifest your desires is achieved basically by changing the way you think and act—change your thoughts, daily habits, and responses, and automatically your experiences and reality will change as well.

Everything you experience in your lifetime, be it a good or bad experience—you have created. No one is to blame for any of your experiences. You don't like hearing this, but it is the truth and that is why you want to learn how to manifest your desires and change your life to a positive loving experience.

Remember again that Rome was not built in a day—nor have you built your life experiences in a day—how to manifest your desires is a quick learn, and once you realize you are able to change your life, you will never look back again. You don't have to spend hours and days or even months manifesting your desires. To begin with just start by "changing the way you think". Whenever there is a confrontation with life, you have a "choice" as how you will act and respond.

FOCUS on the "reality" you want for yourself, it is difficult to begin with, because your mind rolls over with the same negative thought patterns day by day, moment by moment. Firstly concentrate and decide what it is you need to change in your life. What patterns have you created that are causing you to be unhappy? Examples: bad relationships, poverty etc. Once you have established your root cause of suffering, you begin to see what changes need to be made in your life and how to manifest your desires.

Let's say you are poor—your thinking pattern says exactly that "I live in poverty,"—you believe and behave in a living-poor manner. You don't clean yourself, you gain weight, you wear the same clothes day by day, and you never smile. Adjustments now need to be made in order for you to manifest a rich and affluent attitude. This process can be a painful one, as most of us put up a resistance to begin with.

Think of yourself as someone that is a vibrational transmitter like a telephone—you ask and then you receive an answer—this is how you manifest your desires—you put out a thought to the Universe and you get back the answer— the *Law of Attraction*. As you radiate wealth and abundance—your reality will reflect wealth and abundance. In other words behave and believe that this is what you are.

Once you have accepted that *like attracts like*, it will become clear that you can change and create anything. You need to learn to set conditions as well as boundaries. You will automatically know how to manifest your desires—Your conscious and unconscious thoughts become your reality, whether you believe this or not it is true doesn't matter. If you control your thoughts, and focus—whatever you have dreamed of will manifest in your life.

Manifesting Your Heart's Desires

By choosing to learn to *Manifest* you have made the choice to enhance your life and grow Spiritually as well. As you practice these skills you will see your talents and desires begin to strengthen and manifest and some in ways beyond your wildest dreams.

If you practice these steps daily, there are no limits on what you can manifest in your life...*anything is possible*...so choose wisely.

#

Manifesting Meditation

Step One: Breathe Deeply

Begin by taking a nice deep cleansing breath. Breathe in and know that you are breathing in life, energy and abundance.

As you exhale release any stress, strain or tension from your body. Feel it leave you.

Release any thoughts or feelings and just allow yourself to relax.

As you continue to breathe deeply, in and out, in and out, gently shift your focus to your heart center and take a few moments to dwell in this place of peace.

Step Two: Clearly State Your Desire

Imagine a genie has just appeared at your doorstep and grants you three wishes. Anything you desire! What are your three wishes? (Go to your heart and let your heart choose your deepest desire.) If you could only have one wish, which wish would you choose? Remember you must choose only one!

Hint: Select something you want, not something your want to get rid of.

For Example: If my ultimate desire is to be healthy and one of the ways for me to be healthy is to lose weight, my choice would read like this: *I choose to be healthy and physically fit.* Rather than I want to lose weight.

Clearly state your deepest desire. It is helpful to write it down where you can see and read it daily.

Step Three: Visualize Success In Advance

Picture what you desire as if it has already happened, as if it has already manifested for you in your life. Allow your picture to be as vivid as possible...colorful, life like, and very real!

Step Four: Embrace The Feeling

What feeling will having your desire give you?

Feel the feeling you have as you imagine having your desire now.

Hint: Let's use the example *of I desire more abundance in my life*. Ask yourself what feeling do you have as you imagine having all the money you desire? Perhaps you feel rich, wealthy, secure, successful, relieved. Beyond these feelings, what do you feel? Most people report a deeper feeling of peace, freedom. That deeper feeling is what you want to feel. This is known as your *core belief or core value*. *I feel abundantly secure,* is a great affirmation. Do you feel any fears? Be aware if you should. (This may be a place where some extra clearing and cleansing work is needed.)

Step Five: Create An Image

Allow an image to come to you that represents your core feeling. The image can be a place, a person, an object, a color, or shape…

Hint: If your core feeling is having more freedom, an image that may work would be a bird, sailing on the ocean, parasailing, space. If your core feeling is peace an image may be a sunset, a dove, walking in nature, the color pink, a rose.

Step Six: Let It Go!

Let your mind release the intention to your Blessed Higher Self, your Angels, and the Divine.

Hint: This can be done by merely saying to yourself " I now release my desire to the wisdom and power of my Blessed Higher Self and Angels." Allow your mind to shift to your core feeling. As you energize your core feeling, you will manifest your desires, ten fold.

Step Seven: Trust

Trust that you have done all you need to do. Your Blessed Higher Self, your Inner Guide, and your subconscious mind will handle the rest.

I suggest, to begin with, you use these steps every day. Taking a few minutes in the morning when you first awaken is an excellent time to take yourself through these seven steps. Once you become familiar with these steps, you will be able to do them quickly, without needing to write them down.

Feel free to use these steps throughout your day as well. It is an excellent way to keep yourself focused on what is most important to you.

Please let me know how things work out for you. (Contact information is at the end of the book.)

NOTES

CHAPTER ELEVEN

Commitment To Your Spiritual Advancement

BEYOND 2012

God is the foundation of health, prosperity,
wisdom, and eternal joy.
We make our life fulfilled and complete
when we have daily contact with God.
Take the time!
Give your attention to the Almighty Power
that is giving you life, strength, and wisdom.
Pray that unceasing truth flow into your mind,
unceasing strength flow into your body,
unceasing joy fill your Soul.
Take a deep breath—feel the Shakti energy
filling you
through the Crown Chakra
and flowing through your entire being.
Become One with the Spiritual energies
of your Blessed Higher Self.
Know your strength, know your path,
and walk it as a son or daughter of God.

—EAJ

We are magnificent humans emerging from a historic dream that is left behind in the past. We now return to the all-knowing past and *ascend into the future simultaneously.* How long ago was it? How soon will it be upon us again? We awaken, clothed in the Universe as a new species, rising up and becoming one with a new dimension.

As you awaken into the energies of the Fifth Dimension, your old concepts dissolve in the cloud-covered mist of the past, and your fears from the past centuries are gently put to rest.

To live in the Fifth Dimension we cannot have hate, fear, greed, lust or any of the seven deadly sins in our consciousness. Before the transformation occurs, most of civilization will hang on to the illusion of the Third Dimension reality, which is certain to bring death and destruction.

The transformation we need to accomplish in the Fifth Dimension is the act of changing our thoughts. The Indigo, Rainbow, and Crystal children will experience the direct application of the extra strands of DNA, bringing into their bodies the energy from a different dimension. They will become our healers and leaders. (See: *Ascension—Accessing The Fifth Dimension WORKBOOK*)

Many wicked and degenerate ones of this day, think that the only pursuit of any value is to dominate and control others, as they bring them into servitude through threat, pain, and deprivation. All these Souls will soon find their personal goals crushing them completely as they are destroyed by their own selfishness and greed. Those without a true vision will perish in the new energies. They are traveling the path that leads to destruction—or death.

Those without hope, focus, and inner vision will surely perish. This inner vision creates a karmic pattern, an imprint on the Soul that one must fulfill. Dr. Deepak Chopra has said that *whatever you visualize, you actualize*. Without such an inner visual pattern there is no fulfillment, no joy, no accomplishment in life. You simply exist.

The twenty-first century will be remembered as the century when the marriage of science and spirituality is complete. Just as the nineteenth century brought us electricity and indoor plumbing, the twentieth century brought us technology and flight; this century brings us home, back to the harmony of living with and through the wisdom and love of the Blessed Higher Self.

We are returning to using our full Universal body potential. *The Divine Helper,* deep within our subconscious, is reawakened. This is the invisible helper that makes all achievements possible. It gives one the help to master any project, become a perfectionist in any undertaking, or achieve success in any field of endeavor. Just go within and the awareness will come.

The powers of the Divine Helper are limitless so that only miracles are released into the life of one who learns to draw on these energies. Similar to the involuntary actions of our body organs, the Divine Helper is a fabulous inner functioning. It never sleeps. It never tires. It never grows impatient. It is always neutral. With its integrity it seeks to fulfill every desire of man, and it leads everyone to Truth.

It solves every problem, enlightens the mind, and comprehends all things. It is the source of joy, happiness, creativity, and achievement. As it assists one to become perfect in every undertaking and every relationship, the Divine Helper leads one to live the *Laws of the Universe*.

In the Old Testament of the Bible, we are told how faith worked in the lives of the ancients; how Enoch was transformed so that death could not touch him; how Noah built the ark through his faith in the *promises* given to him. *Abraham lived by the inner promise* that opened to him, as did Sarah.

In the thirteenth and fifteenth verses of the eleventh chapter of Hebrews, it states that all these Patriarchs, that is except Enoch, died in faith, of never having realized their promises, but having seen them 'afar off.' If these Patriarchs had *not* seen their promise as only a possibility, a promise of the future, *as afar off,* they would have been able to bring it into reality. This scripture of *afar off* is tremendous.

Many Patriarchs of old or any living Soul since, who has held the Promise of God within, failed because they placed their wishes and desires afar off. Many will say, "Yes, well, perhaps in my next life." But it's different now because whatever you think about, you can manifest quickly. At this time, and you may have already noticed, whatever you focus on will happen. The information and energy you ask for or desire will come in to manifestation instantaneously—*this is the gift beyond 2012.*

In the twentieth century, many teachers such as Louise Hay and Dr. Deepak Chopra realized the interconnection of body, mind, and Universe; the psychic sixth sense; and the physical, expressed through synchronicities, and other mystic correspondences. These teachers understand that a deep transformation of the human psyche is underway and show us how to stay healthy, balanced, and wise during this transformation.

For thousands of years, our extrasensory abilities, used for so long by our indigenous ancestors with reverence and respect to explore and learn, have been diverted by our priestly bureaucrats into various Spiritual dead ends. Everything preached is dogma, endlessly repeated, and almost no one has first hand experiences of the transpersonal dimensions.

As long as people are taught to fear and shy away from their *true inner selves*, nothing new can be discovered and learned. Yet the truth is always there, waiting for us to access it just on the other side of the mirror. This is the lesson of the seeker's path: to experience the direct, transpersonal, and transformative experience of the sacred realms. We are becoming true visionaries and creators of our future.

We are currently experiencing the beginning of the Apocalypse, a word that has familiar destructive connotations but that is also defined as *revealing* or *uncovering*.

As a negative example, the Apocalypse represents the destruction of previous forms of thought and ways of being; as a positive, it represents a momentous event—the coming of the Self into conscious realization. The experience of Oneness with all things.

The true *State of Being*, the complete expression of our being, merges both the conscious and unconscious levels. Our limited ego dreads the coming of the complete Universal Self because it doesn't want to do the work, let go of the past, or put the time in to create change. This 'little self' would rather stay put, cling to the old, or die trying. As a result, mankind has reached a crossroads.

This new world harmonizes science, spirituality, religion, and history. The knowledge comes together to form a single higher vibration and focus on greater wisdom. When this occurs, miracles happen. As you increasingly understand what the Fifth Dimension brings, you will realize that *it is you* who writes the script. You are the one who determines how this transformative experience will play out in your life.

The more you assist one another and release the extremely violent portrayal that the Earth is on a path of destruction, the more joyful you will feel. You can create an inner peace and a Divine harmony among all beings, both on the planet and off. Although the Earth must go through a difficult period both geologically as well as with mankind, you can begin to transform your fear into the energy of anticipation.

We are to be lifted up into this glorious new world—*no Spiritual being will be left behind*. As the 144,000 petals of the chakras open, our foreheads are marked with the Light of the Universal energy coming through and awakening our Souls from deep within. This is the vision of Light marked on the forehead, the white seal as mentioned in Scripture; the mark that will be brought forward. As we meditate on the chakras, our Third Eye glows in the darkness, allowing the angels and beings in the other dimensions to recognize us, and pulls us along the path to a deathless future: a future of service to the Divine, creating our good, and working on our continual evolvement into the higher dimensions.

Why commit to your personal Spiritual advancement?
To create a new life, new understanding, expansion of love, elimination of fear, hurt, illness, and unbalance. A new world is coming, and it's coming for you and me. It's just around the bend. This new world emerges without any type of negative aspect; a world of love beyond love; an exciting world of the constantly emerging Spiritual energies.

This book is full of wisdom, exercises, and information to help you develop the invisible part of Self, and raise your vibration up to new levels. You are working with your Universal Body, the Fifth Dimension frequencies, and your past, present, and future! There are many marvelous and magical benefits when you commit to your Spiritual advancement. Begin now to create the fulfilled, balanced, and joyful life you deserve!

NOTES

NOTES

HEALING AND CLEARING EXERCISES TO PREPARE TO SET A CONDITION OR MANIFEST

Healing and Clearing Exercises

Suggestion: For background music use *ARDAS* – Crimson Series.

IF YOU GET SPACEY – STOP. If you get disoriented, stop, and if you have any questions, stop. These energies can open you up very quickly, so it's important that you stay in tune and aware of yourself and what's going on round you.

MANTRA: Do anytime before you do these exercises; it will clear your aura and the space around you and it also focuses on the God within you. Use some soft, spiritual music in the background

Ong Na Mo

Guru Devi Na Mo

Ong = the Divine working within me

Na Mo = I bow to Thee reverently

Guru Devi = is a Divine teacher – a favorite Yogi = you are asking the Divine wisdom to awaken within you.

It is very important that you ask for the Divine to be with you when you do any type of Spiritual Intensive work or meditation.

Bring your hands into a prayer like position and tuck your arms in. This stimulates a meridian point within and will take you to a state of neutrality.

Ong na mo
Guru devi na mo

Remember you are calling on the Divine to be with you – feel it – sense it – be aware of the moving and flowing energies. Now – we will do this three times – as it is best to do this three to five times each time you begin your sessions.

Okay, breathe in deeply, slowly exhale.
Ad guru Nemaha
Jihad guru Nemaha
Sat guru Nemaha
Shri devi guru Nemaha
Place your hands flat on your thighs. Begin with some deep breathing.

Begin working with the breath, and a very important breath that you will want to master is known as the "Complete Breath." The complete breath is very simple. Just put your right hand across your navel, and when you inhale, your stomach will expand. When you exhale, you pull the stomach in. Keep working with this exercise a few minutes. This will clear your charkas of negative energies. Really push the stomach out as it maximizes the amount of oxygen or energy that you bring into your body. Pull the stomach back in as you exhale and maximize the amount of waste released by exhalation. You also push the diaphragm gently up to massage the internal organs.

This exercise creates a very powerful breath. If you are a businessperson under a lot of stress with high-level meetings, this breath works. It will relax you, indeed, it cannot help but relax you, because breath can control brain wave patterns.

Do the breath work for three to eleven minutes.

This is called the *control of the Prana*. Keep your body straight allow your diaphragm to do the work, not your shoulders but your diaphragm, inhale and exhale through your nose. Nice deep breaths, it is one of the simplest and healthiest things you can do. Really pull your stomach in when you exhale. This gives you a high concentration of oxygen into your system. Most people breathe using the upper third of their lung; this technique will make you very tense. It stimulates the glands to secrete and you can get an artificial high off of it. The thing is most people are running on this and they don't even realize it. Nice deep breathing, the average is ten to twelve breaths per minute.

Slow the breath down. Your first goal is to move to eight times per minute. Then to six times a minute, and then when the breath is four times or less a minute, then you will be able to access what is known as the alpha-theta level of consciousness by merely using your breath. Keep working with it, feel how good it feels to breathe deeply. This allows you to maximize the prana or life force energy that you pull in through your lungs. You are not just breathing in oxygen, you are pulling in life-force energy. In physics they call this zero point energy or latent energy. It may seem foreign, and that's okay, that's normal. This is the way we are supposed to breathe, but we don't.

Feel yourself pulling that life source in. Feel it moving throughout your body from your lungs, traveling through the veins, the arteries, the capillaries, through the nervous system. See it traveling throughout your entire body. Run this energy from the top of your head to the tips of your toes.

Continue for just a few more minutes. Visualize your breath traveling throughout your lungs, throughout your entire body. This is a great technique when you are blasted with negative energy. This is a technique that can stop a sleepless night or intense headaches. It will blow the energy out of yourself, out of your aura. Any unprocessed energy will leave you. What many don't realize is that this works. You receive negative energy daily in your workplace and when you interact with people also. That's why you can use these techniques for many problems that you may have because there is energy flowing and acting up between us all the time. You need to dissipate and clear that energy out. Did you ever go into a meeting with someone and they were bouncing off the wall? They are breathing fire. Before long you are tense and upset. Why? Because you are pulling in part of that energy and making it your own. You need to get the message they are trying to convey, but don't bring in their negative energy with it. If you do, use this technique to get rid of it.

Keep working with it. You want to become a master of this breath technique. No matter how long you have to practice, you will want to master it. Really pull the diaphragm in.

Some people may feel meditative when you do this. You may feel a tingling in parts of your body. The important thing is that your back be kept straight. Let yourself really get into it and listen to the sound of your breathing, listen to the breath as it comes into the nose and down into the lungs. Just listening to the sound of your breath is a meditation on its own. So we have already covered several meditations here that you can do as one like we are doing now, or you can break it up into different parts.

Continue to just breathe deep and relax and if you need to stretch your legs out, do so. Listen to the sound of your breath, focus and go inside, listen to that breath. It almost is music of its own. Now exhale, inhale deeply and hold and slowly exhale. Inhale deeply and hold again, slowly exhale. Inhale deeply one final time. Slowly exhale. Very slowly open your eyes.

Now we will take this exercise to the next level.

BREATH OF FIRE EXERCISE

It's called *Breath of Fire*. You inhale quickly, exhale quickly—it's the exact same exercise we were doing only at a faster pace. Work at your own pace here, but the speed you want to work up to is two-and-one-half cycles per second.

It's very easy, it's challenging fun and you may like it. It will warm you up. It is not a clinical hyperventilation. Studies on this technique have determined that if you do this through your mouth you may fall over and pass out or faint. Doing this through your nose does not induce hyperventilation. Breathe through your nose, and I am sure you will want to practice this every day when you go home. However it will do many magical things for you. This technique is very cleansing to your whole body. Put your hand on your stomach, inhale and begin Breath of Fire. Remember to work at your own pace. One minute.

Keep going. Inhale deeply and hold, and then begin your long complete breath. Nice deep breathing. Nice long deep breathing. One minute.

Now breathe in deeply and begin Breath of Fire. One

Exhale and the stomach deflates; inhale and the stomach inflates. Be very powerful with this breath. Be strong and get stronger with it. Now, inhale deeply, and begin the long, deep breathing. You are using muscles that you don't use a whole lot. This should be taught in elementary schools and high schools.

Inhale deeply—begin Breath of Fire. Keep going—you're doing great. This will give you energy and it stimulates the third chakra and helps to balance the third chakra. Also, it stimulates the Pituitary in your brain, so let your stomach do the work.

Inhale deeply and hold, then slowly exhale.

Build up slowly, from one to eleven minutes.

If you feel some body pain, stop and relax. You may be holding some negative energy and need to process that through anyway. Remember this is shot-gunning any negative energy.

THE GOLDEN RING OF FIRE FOR CLEARING AND PURIFICATION

The Ring of Fire is a sacred visualization used by Yogi Masters and the Shaman. These great Yogi's have brought this meditation up to higher levels to help us create abundance, eliminate resistance, negativity and fear of receiving and the power to strengthen our self esteem, spiritual energies, and belief in our work.

To prepare the body to receive the *Golden Ring of Fire* and purification, begin with reciting the mantra, Sat Nam—with God. Sit up straight in a chair, have both feet flat on the floor, take three deep breaths. Then begin by turning your head to the left and say "Sat," then swing the head back to the center. Take another breath and turn the head to the right, saying "Nam," then move the head back to the center again. Repeat this process, gaining an even flow and smooth rhythm, for sixteen times, exact.

Now take three more deep breaths. Begin the yoga practice of the *Breath of Fire*. Breathe in fast and heavy, in the abdomen, not the shallow lungs. Move the abdomen in and out, like you are pushing down. In-out-in-out-in-out–in-out, quickly. Try to create an energy flow. This is not easy, but necessary to loosen all of your negativity, and stuck, un-moveable energy. Do this for up to eleven minutes. Begin with one minute, and consider yourself an expert if you can do this for three minutes. There are aches and pains with this exercise, especially in the lower back. This is where you store the energy of fear for the future, fear of lack of security. Just breathe and move it all out.

Now it's time to begin the purification exercise of the Golden Ring of Fire.

Visualize a golden ring of light, with a yellow, orange, blue, and greenish flame and see this light spinning around in a clockwise circle. This circle of light moves down to you from the Twelfth Chakra, above your aura field, and your Blessed Higher Self. As your Aura merges within this light - see it surrounded with the golden white light and the light rays flowing through your Aura. Notice where there may be black spots, similar to sunspots. These are called your "field of resistance."

Once the rays are flowing though you, begin to move the black spots of resistance toward your left side and out of your body. Repeat this Affirmation:

I stand within the Strength
Of the Ring of Fire and Purification
I allow this golden light to flow through me
It flows continual—with no beginning and no
end
I purify and release any and all energies
That may prevent the flow of abundance in my
life
That may prevent the flow security in my life
That may prevent the flow of good health in my
life
I claim my full Personhood
And release any and all negativity NOW.

Take three deep breaths, and see the black spots leaving your body through the left side as you exhale. See the negativity merging into the light rays within your Ring of Fire, to purify them, changing their vibration levels to positive forces. Take another deep breath and be sure you are clear within and without. Continue with the last part of the Affirmation as you allow the light rays to flow through you for one minute.

Then visualize a ring of fire above your head in a huge circle, like a large wreath. See it—then bring it down over your body—to burn away negativity—see this ring coming down over your head, your shoulders, your torso, your hips and thighs, your legs, your feet; Throw it down into the center of the earth. Know that this *Ring Of Fire* is burning away your fears, doubts, insecurities, leaving a void for new and positive thoughts and actions for you.

See yourself standing in the Golden Light flame until you feel a completeness and Inner Peace. Begin the mantra, *"I am healthy, whole, and complete. Thank you, Spirit."*

NOW – Continue to Meditate, keeping your eyes closed! Begin to work/spin your Chakras, up to at least the Eighth Chakra. Then wrap yourself thoroughly in White Light.

Visualize the Circle of Light, as your vibration should be higher now. Then bring your Self and your desires into the Circle. Sit with that vision; notice what is happening around you. Are colors changing? What are you experiencing within yourself? Make statements or visualize the outcome of your Desire. DO NOT even think about or worry about how you will get there. Leave that all up to the Universe.

You are complete with this extremely powerful meditation. You have actually moved energy, as long as you did your inner work without obstacles and worry. That's the trick because when you doubt yourself, you create blocks and obstacles.

Instead of thinking "If it's right it will come to me," think "This is here, and I am in gratitude of the outcome."

To create a full abundance, we must allow the clear flow of all things, including *trust, knowledge, and love.*

#

You can work with my guided meditation, *"The Chakras and Your Body,"* for that part of this exercise. The music played by Richard Shulman will aid in clearing.

Now that you are clear, the creativity begins. To start this process, *put yourself in the direct center* of the Ring of Fire—the EYE. It is colorless, or transparent black, representing emptiness of thought. Be still, very still. Be Still and KNOW that I am GOD

Listen to the silence. As you listen, remaining clear of thought, begin to visualize what you would like to bring into your life. See it, feel it or think it, whatever is your personal process. Imagine this coming to you as clearly as you can. When you feel it fully created, put it inside a pink/violet circle of spinning energy and allow it to float out into the Universe. Release the thought form and have faith that it will manifest in your life in Divine Order. Have faith in God's love and your unconditional love for yourself.

The work is done, and the manifestation will follow, in its own time and in its own way. Remember, God works in strange ways with you and through you. Opportunities come forward, new people come to support your wishes, and your life takes a new turn upward on the Spiral. Realize that you cannot rush these energies. Allow yourself to feel that your present circumstances are only temporary and take as many steps as you can, now, to bring the manifestation into reality. That means that if you get an inner suggestion to call someone regarding a desire or project, don't allow fear of rejection to stop you. Go for it! Do not allow anything in your life or space to go untouched or unused. *Stay in the FLOW.*

ABOUT THE AUTHOR

Elizabeth Joyce

Born as one of two sets of identical twins, Elizabeth Joyce has been psychic since birth. Named one of the *World's Greatest Psychics* (Citadel Press, 2004), and now one of *The Top 100 American Psychics* (2014), she is profiled in twelve books. She is a Spiritual healer and gives personal psychic readings worldwide. Ms. Joyce is a professional Astrologer, Spiritual Counselor, Energy Healer, Medium and Clairvoyant who interprets dreams and teaches the new energies of the Fifth Dimension.

Elizabeth has been a writer and columnist for thirty years and is currently writing Astrology columns for *Wisdom Magazine* and *Toti Publishing*. Her articles have appeared in the *New York Daily News* and the *New York Times*.

Elizabeth has been teaching metaphysical classes for the past twenty-five years. In 1986, just before the Harmonic Convergence, she was blessed to be initiated into the Hopi Tribe by Grandfather. She was just nominated into the 2010 Edition of the *Stanford Who's Who In Metaphysics* for her Spiritual healing work and focus on Community Service.

Elizabeth has studied with Margaret Stettner, Indira Ivey, Louise Hay, Dr. Deepak Chopra, Yogi Bhajan, Marc Tremblay, and Ammachi; Elizabeth has also trained with Dr. Eric Pearl and is a Reconnective Healer, and she is a licensed minister.

Her TV Appearances include *Unsolved Mysteries, Beyond Chance,* and *The Psychic Detectives* as well as several talk shows. Elizabeth has done hundreds of radio shows and is featured on *Coast to Coast AM* with George Noory.

She is currently a regular guest on *The X-Zone* with Rob McConnell.

Her website is one of the top-rated in her field.

Elizabeth facilitates her own *Developing Your Intuitive Awareness* classes and Divine Sittings, using the Divine Seals and Spiritual Chakras from her book *Ascension—Accessing The Fifth Dimension WORKBOOK.*

Elizabeth is located in Doylestown, PA (Bucks County)

Listen to Elizabeth Joyce on
BBSRadio.com/LetsFindOut
Mondays at 6:00 PM Pacific
And 9:00 PM Eastern

Website: *www.new-visions.com*
Phone: 201-934-8986—24 hour service

E-Mail: Elizabeth.joyce.email@gmail.com